WALTER
Brueggemann

THE
THREAT OF

LIFE

Sermons on
Pain, Power, and
edited by Weakness
Charles L. Campbell

FORTRESS PRESS
MINNEAPOLIS

THE THREAT OF LIFE
Sermons on Pain, Power, and Weakness

Cover design: Brad Norr
Text Design: David Lott

Library of Congress Cataloging-in-Publication Data

Brueggemann, Walter.
    The threat of life : sermons on pain, power, and weakness / Walter
Brueggemann ; edited by Charles Campbell.
        p.   cm.
    Includes bibliographical references.
    ISBN 0-8006-2975-2 (alk. paper)
    1. Sermons, American.   I. Campbell, Charles.   II. Title.
BV4253.B78   1996
252—dc20   96-32291
                                                                     CIP

Manufactured in the U.S.A.   AF 1-2975
    00   99   98   97   96   1   2   3   4   5   6   7   8   9   10

Contents

Part Three: Texts from the Writings

Part Four: New Testament Texts with Old Testament Allusions

Preface

I am glad to offer these sermons as an act of solidarity with those who are "handlers of the word of God," preachers and not "peddlers." I shall be pleased if these sermons serve to strengthen my colleagues in their demanding work. I hope, moreover, that the interpretive lines I have pursued here—the linkages of Old Testament and New Testament, the epicenter of the Bible for the church, the enterprise of speech as generative of life, and the capacity of the gospel to give life in a world bent on death—are suggestive and supportive of those who preach and those who listen. Clearly such accents are not new ones, but the present attention to the themes of pluralism and plurivocity, rhetoric, intertextuality, the Jewishness of the Christian faith, the baptismal scandal of the church, "news" in the public square—all these indicate that pastors are now required to find their own freedom, buoyancy, and courage with and through this text. Entrusted to us is this text so long and so well trusted by our mothers and fathers who have, in every season, preached, listened, and acted with a simple, defiant courage that the world thought foolish.

My first word of thanks is to Charles Campbell in whom I delight as a colleague. It has not taken us long to discover that we are on the same wavelength concerning interpretive issues. For that reason, I dared approach Campbell about helping me with this volume of sermons. In response, he has been consistently supportive, wise in his counsel, and thoughtful in his critical editorial work.

My second word of thanks is to my three "usual suspects." Tempie Alexander persists in doing my secretarial work patiently, quickly, generously, and competently. In these sermons, she has had a series of demanding deadlines. Marshall Johnson, Director of Fortress Press, warrants my great appreciation for his willingness to take on yet another manuscript of mine, which is in a rather odd genre. Mary Miller Brueggemann has lived with these sermons and through their preaching, coping with my sometimes despairing faith, my excessive exhilaration, and my seasons of fatigue that go along with costly preaching.

My final thanks is to the numerous preachers of many sorts who have granted me the privilege of preaching in their pulpits and welcoming me to do so. Such invitations and gestures of sharing are acts of deep trust and friendship, and I am appreciative of that generosity and risk. Of course these preachers—and many others—are my most intimate allies in the sermons I offer here. While maintaining intellectual credibility is important to me, it is increasingly clear to me that the church and its preaching is my natural habitat. I have no doubt that preaching is now a most demanding work in a pluralistic church, and a most urgent work in a culture that is in profound crisis. I dare to imagine that the church will not find its way into fresh fidelity nor will our culture find its way into serious humanness, apart from faithful, courageous preaching.

Walter Brueggemann

Foreword

O ne question that regularly stirs up spirited debate among seminary students and pastors is, How does one preach from the Old Testament? Among many Christians today there is a proper concern for the integrity of the Hebrew Scriptures. (Some even reject the term "Old Testament" as derogatory.) At the same time, however, there are widely divergent views on how the Old Testament is faithfully used in a Christian sermon. These views range from those which insist on the self-sufficiency of Old Testament texts as sources for Christian preaching to those which require a strong christological move at the heart of every sermon. And, of course, there are many positions in between.

This issue arises with some urgency for preachers who regularly use the lectionary. Indeed, the compilers of the Revised Common Lectionary have themselves struggled with the relationship between the Old and New Testament lections; changes in the Old Testament readings represent the most obvious recent revisions. Reflecting contemporary disagreements, the compilers of the lectionary have arrived at a compromise, offering the church, during Ordinary Time at least, the option of (1) following semicontinuous readings from the Old Testament, which are not intentionally related to the New Testament texts or (2) using more traditional Old Testament lections, which are governed by the Gospel readings.[1]

While creating more options for preachers, this compromise regarding the Old Testament lections only further complicates

---

1. *The Revised Common Lectionary* (Nashville: Abingdon Press, 1992); see esp. 11, 77–78.

another question that preachers frequently ask: Should I focus on one lectionary text, or should I try to preach "intertextually," relating two or more of the lectionary readings? And if I choose to preach intertextually, how do I go about it? To preach from the lectionary, then, is to encounter not only the dilemma of preaching from the Old Testament, but also the related issue of intertextual preaching.

Over the past few years, Walter Brueggemann and I have periodically discussed these issues, often indirectly through students taking both his Old Testament courses and my preaching classes. While our theoretical discussions have been stimulating, I have found that Brueggemann's own sermons provide a more helpful way of addressing these concerns. Theoretical reflection can be valuable, to be sure. However, it is in the actual practice of preaching that decisions about these matters are made and embodied.[2] Brueggemann's sermons are particularly rich in this regard.

In all of the sermons in this volume, Old Testament texts play an important role. Most of the sermons are based primarily on a text from the Old Testament, while a few demonstrate different ways of using Old Testament material when the primary text is from the New. What is fascinating, however, is the variety of ways in which Brueggemann manages to maintain the integrity of the Old Testament texts while at the same time preaching sermons that are distinctively Christian and unequivocally addressed to "the baptized." There are no artificial, forced moves to Jesus in these sermons (an approach that Brueggemann regularly criticizes in his classes). Nevertheless, the sermons exhibit a deep christological and ecclesiolog-

2. For recent books on preaching from the Old Testament, see Elizabeth Achtemeier, *Preaching from the Old Testament* (Louisville: Westminster/John Knox Press, 1989); Donald E. Gowan, *Reclaiming the Old Testament for the Christian Pulpit* (Atlanta: John Knox Press, 1980); John C. Holbert, *Preaching Old Testament: Proclamation and Narrative in the Hebrew Bible* (Nashville: Abingdon Press, 1991). For a recent collection of sermons largely from Old Testament texts, see James L. Crenshaw, *Trembling at the Threshold of a Biblical Text* (Grand Rapids, Mich.: Wm. B. Eerdmans, 1994). The differences between Brueggemann's sermons and Crenshaw's are striking and worthy of study.

ical sensitivity, which surfaces formally in brief allusions, recurring patterns and motifs, and specific "intertextual" connections. One comes away from the sermons not with a "Christologized" Old Testament, but rather with a deepened appreciation for the Jewishness of Jesus and the embeddedness of the gospel within the larger biblical narrative. Brueggemann thus offers a distinctive approach to preaching from the Old Testament, which may prove helpful to many preachers.

In addition, many of Brueggemann's sermons provide examples of intertextual lectionary preaching—preaching that employs two or more of the lectionary texts. Although not uncritical of the lectionary, Brueggemann is generally a lectionary preacher, as the sermons in this volume indicate. Frequently he uses multiple lections in a sermon. Here Brueggemann's appreciation for both the sweep of the biblical narrative and the liturgical context of the readings enables him to make rich connections among the biblical texts, which should prove suggestive for lectionary preachers.

While helpful with regard to preaching from the Old Testament and the lectionary, Brueggemann's sermons also invite study with regard to their content, form, and hermeneutical method. The most striking thing about the sermons is their content: God. The sermons are saturated with God; they are passionate about God. They are fundamentally theological sermons. At a time when personal experience and the therapeutic model often dominate the pulpit, Brueggemann keeps our attention on the biblical story and the God whose identity that story renders. Brueggemann unapologetically proclaims the "odd" God of the Bible, who is never some general divinity or universal principle, but an intrusive, particular God who is active in the world. And Brueggemann invites the church to become an odd people, a countercultural community, whose identity is formed in relation to this peculiar God.

The form of the sermons is consistent with this focus on the God of the Bible. The biblical text itself generally shapes the movement of the sermon. In fact, in some ways the form is reminiscent of older, expository sermons. In many instances, for example, Brueggemann simply walks through a particular text. With

Brueggemann's sermons, however, unlike some forms of expository preaching, one rarely feels bogged down in extraneous exegetical details, and one rarely senses an artificial separation between "exposition" and "application." In part, this engaging expository style results from Brueggemann's social-literary approach to Scripture, which brings the social dimensions of the text into play while focusing primarily on the movement of the canonical text itself. Brueggemann's sensitivity to the social character of the Bible, his creative insights into the fundamental drama of the biblical texts, his helpful use of biblical characters, and his subtle employment of anachronism all contribute to an expository preaching that has a dramatic and contemporary ring. Indeed, Brueggemann's sermons model a kind of dramatic, expository preaching which is not only possible today but appropriate for the biblically illiterate church.

Brueggemann's hermeneutical method also contributes to his distinctive, expository style. In his sermons Brueggemann seeks to "read" the world through the strange, old texts of the Bible. He engages in a task of radical redescription. That is, he seeks to redescribe—or, as he might put it, retextualize—the contemporary world through the Bible. The biblical texts serve as multiple lenses through which Brueggemann repeatedly seeks to see and interpret the world. Here Brueggemann reverses liberal attempts to fit the Bible into a purportedly wider modern framework in order to make it relevant. Instead, for Brueggemann, the "world of the Bible" provides the primary frame of reference into which the contemporary world is incorporated.

Reading the world through the biblical texts, Brueggemann not only speaks to the church about theological matters but also addresses critical public concerns—social, political, and economic. In so doing, he reveals the fallacy of David Buttrick's recent assertion that biblical theology contributes something to preaching that is both past-tense and nonprophetic.[3] Contrary to Buttrick's criticism, Brueggemann's biblical-theological preaching is both con-

3. David Buttrick, *A Captive Voice: The Liberation of Preaching* (Louisville: Westminster/John Knox Press, 1994), 9–12.

temporary and prophetic. In Brueggemann's sermons the strange, old texts begin to sound as public and current as today's newspaper. And through them the world of the newspaper is redescribed. Brueggemann thus demonstrates that "the world of the Bible" can indeed capture our imagination and reshape our common life. He beckons us to enter that world and be transformed.

Charles L. Campbell
Columbia Theological Seminary

PART
ONE
Torah Texts

CHAPTER 1

A Demanding Long-Term Miracle

Genesis 17:1-10

When Abram was ninety-nine years old, the LORD appeared to Abram, and said to him, "I am God Almighty; walk before me, and be blameless. And I will make my covenant between me and you, and will make you exceedingly numerous." Then Abram fell on his face; and God said to him, "As for me, this is my covenant with you: You shall be the ancestor of a multitude of nations. No longer shall your name be Abram, but your name shall be Abraham; for I have made you the ancestor of a multitude of nations. I will make you exceedingly fruitful; and I will make nations of you, and kings shall come from you. I will establish my covenant between me and you, and your offspring after you throughout their generations, for an everlasting covenant, to be God to you and to your offspring after you. And I will give to you, and to your offspring after you, the land where you are now an alien, all the land of Canaan, for a perpetual holding; and I will be their God."

God said to Abraham, "As for you, you shall keep my covenant, you and your offspring after you throughout their generations. This is my covenant, which you shall keep, between me and you and your offspring after you: Every male among you shall be circumcised."

Texts: Genesis 17:1-10, 15-19
Psalm 105:1-11
Romans 4:16-25
Mark 8:31-39

The Bible regularly confesses more than it understands. It claims more than can ever be explained. Its exuberant, unrestrained overstatement is an embarrassment to us. The Bible dares to assert that a miracle from God stands central to our faith and at the bottom of life. In our recent scientific period, say two hundred years, well-educated people have tried to dislodge this claim of miracle or at least make it marginal. In the face of our modernity, either sophisticated or obscurantist, the Bible is unembarrassed about its assertion that, at root, a very particular miracle is at the center of our world.

We are not speaking of a big, spectacular miracle, but a little, local one. We can name it, and we cling to it tenaciously. It goes like this—in its embarrassment. Our faith-father Abraham was a very old man. His wife Sarah, our faith-mother, was equally old and they could not have a child. All their hopes, all God's promises, the whole story, hinged on a child to inherit, but none was given. Abraham did have Ishmael, born of a surrogate mother, and old, almost cynical Abraham was prepared to let this Ishmael, be his rightful and only heir, because there was no other on the horizon, or even possible.

But, as the story goes, God has more faith, more resilience, more confidence in a possible future than does Abraham or Sarah. Then, inexplicably, this yearned-for, unexpected, desperately wanted baby is born, not of normal human circumstance, but of the power and fidelity of God. This birth is an event defying explanation, resisting reason. Abraham and Sarah and all of us are thrown back from reason and understanding to the more elemental responses of wonder, astonishment, amazement, gratitude, praise, and laughter. In that moment of birth and thanksgiving Israel has broken free from all

This sermon was preached at Nassau Presbyterian Church, Princeton, N.J. The texts are from the lectionary for the Second Sunday in Lent.

the bonds of reasonable control and technical prediction. There is only the dance of faith that does not ask for explanation. From that moment on, Israel lives by the inexplicable that evokes gratitude. What Israel sees of God's oddness is not craziness, but powerful faithfulness which can keep promises against all odds. Biblical faith is grounded in God's capacity to keep promises. In that moment Israel comes to know everything that needs to be known about God and about the world and about us. We live in a world of surplus surprises that outrun our capacity to control or predict or explain.

From that treasured gift wondrously given, Israel's lyrical imagination takes off. It sings, it extrapolates, it exaggerates, it generalizes. The God who can give a baby can give everything. The God who can work this new life can work all new life in every circumstance. The bounds of possibility are broken. This is not confidence in human, technical capacity or ingenuity or wisdom, but amazement about the power of life at work beyond our management. Israel sings and dances about the God of Abraham and Sarah, about the God who makes promises and keeps them, who keeps covenant and gives land. Israel in Psalm 105 dares to reread its entire history as a tale of surprising gifts wondrously given. Every aspect of life is now set to lyrics that invite celebration and amazement.

The most eloquent extrapolation of this miraculous baby is given by Paul in Romans 4. In this exotic, lyrical passage, Paul uses all the words we expect Paul to use—faith, promise, grace (v. 16). Then Paul gets quite concrete (vv. 19-20) in telling what it was like for this frail old man and this fruitless woman to notice their hopeless, wrinkled bodies that had no vitality and to be amazed at their gift beyond reason. Between Paul's regular theological vocabulary and his historical reminiscence, Paul utters what must be one of the most remarkable assertions in the Bible: This God in whom Israel believes, "gives life to the dead and calls into existence the things that do not exist" (v. 17).

The lyrical quality of this affirmation is surely a confession beyond understanding, a claim beyond explanation. Liberal rationalists have been busy getting rid of miracles because they violate our control. Reactionaries have had a few select miracles they massage—creation instead of evolution, virgin birth, physical resurrection—but Paul's rhetoric blows both liberal reticence and reactionary selectivity out of the water: "gives life to the dead. Calls into existence the things that do not exist." This entire lyrical claim comes from one baby born to an old couple. In the unexpected birth of little Isaac, God has made outrageous promises of well-being for all time to come. Paul and the whole church are custodians of that outrageous promise. And, along the way, we identify hints and glimpses and oddities where the impossible power of God has overcome our tightly disciplined, fearfully guarded notion of what is possible.

Thus a dialogue is set up in our faith. One voice says, "Can you imagine!" The other voice answers, "Yes, but." Abraham, old, almost cynical Abraham was filled with "Yes, but." Yes, but I am very old. Yes, but she is not pregnant. Yes, but we only have Ishmael. It is the naked voice of the gospel that counters his tiredness. Can you imagine a new son born right then? Can you imagine a covenant kept to countless generations to come? Can you imagine land given to landless people? Not: can you implement it, can you plan it, can you achieve it?—only: can you entrust possibilities to God that go beyond your own capacity for control and fabrication?

The New Testament is not different. The people around Jesus are filled with the grudging hesitance of "yes, but." Jesus comes and says, Can you imagine a dinner for all? Can you imagine a blind boy to see? Can you imagine a prodigal welcomed home? Can you imagine a Pharisee reborn into childlike innocence? Can you imagine lepers healed, widows cared for, poor people made first-class citizens? Of course, it was judged impossible, but Jesus ran powerfully ahead of such fear.

In our day, today, "Yes, but" is powerful and usually wins. "Yes, but" makes us sane, sober, prudent, competent. But it can also drive us to despair, fatigue, cynicism, and even brutality. If you can imagine a baby born to such a failed family:

- Can you imagine a world of valued old people? Yes, but consider the costs and the overwhelming statistics.

- Can you imagine a Latin America unencumbered by imperial domination? Yes, but Castro is so close.
- Can you imagine a missile-free Europe? Yes, but Russia has such powerful group forces.
- Can you imagine a new world of food for all? Yes, but our standard of living resists such sharing.
- Can you imagine a rehabilitated marriage? Yes, but he or she always. . . .

The list goes on, because Israel's lyrical imagination is free and unquenchable. God brings into existence that which does not exist. Did you know that the Bible never uses the word *create* with a human subject? We may "make" or "form" or "fabricate," but only God creates, only God works a genuine new possibility, a new thing beyond our expectations and our extrapolations. It belongs to the mystery and holiness of God to call to be that which is not yet. Because this is God's world, the world is not closed, either by our hopes or by our fears.

When we have our lives governed by "Yes, but," by our proud capacity to control or our fearful need to control, we resist God's power for newness. We deny God's freedom to give gifts. We end the song, we stop the lyric, we deny the truth of memory, and we only hold on grimly. Holding on grimly is an act of atheism, governed by "Yes, but," believing there is no more than what we can explain, no more than what we can control, manage, and predict.

Those of us who gather around these texts and these powerful memories keep alive in our lives the terrible, unsettling transition between "Yes, but" and "Can you imagine?" Most of the time, "Yes, but" wins. But by God's powerful grace, the "Yes, but" of our resistance is broken. Newness appears; we can sing songs, unembarrassed, songs about miracles.

The lectionary committee has done a hard and mean thing to us. It has juxtaposed to these powerful texts a Gospel story in which Jesus says, "I must die, I must be crucified" (Mark 8:31). Then Jesus, in the face of Peter's resistance, gives us a powerful, frightening invitation:

If anyone would follow me, let them . . . take up their cross. . . .
Those who lose their life for my sake . . . will save it.

(Mark 8:34-35)

It is at best odd to speak about demanding discipleship in the context of such powerful promises as we have just considered. The Bible, however, has known about this juxtaposition all along. God's incredible newness can be resisted by our capacity and desire to save our lives. We do not want to turn loose. We do not want to relinquish. All our "Yes, buts" are designed to keep control, so that we are not placed in jeopardy. We keep death at bay by our determination. Our long series of "Yes, buts" are designed to resist the Gospel—not only its costs, but its terrible surprises.

Abraham, our father in faith, is not the only one for whom God did staggering things. He is also an invitation to believe and trust and risk and relinquish. He is the one who was fully convinced that God was able to do what God had promised (Rom. 4:21). Abraham was, in an awesome moment of faith, prepared to receive God's newness that was against all probability, but that set his life utterly new. Abraham might have said "Yes, but." He might have, if he were embarrassed and sophisticated. Such faith, however, is not enacted by those who are embarrassed. It is modeled by the daring who sing songs, who receive gifts, who make journeys, who confess more than they understand and who claim more than they explain. Faith is enacted by those who trust God who imagines well beyond our resistant presuppositions. Such imagination requires a dying and yields utterly new life.

No one could have foreseen how long-term and how demanding was the birth of Isaac. That single birth is long term even until now. It is demanding because its newness requires many relinquishments—economic, intellectual, religious, political. It requires especially relinquishing that "Yes, but" which hinders our singing. What it demands, however, is more than matched by what it gives —newness, things that do yet exist. We would not have thought that this birth would lead to such possibility and such demand. But then, Isaac is no ordinary miracle. And the God who birthed Isaac is no conventional God. This God intends us no conventional life.

CHAPTER

2

Taking a Second, Painful Look

Genesis 45:3-15

Joseph said to his brothers, "I am Joseph. Is my father still alive?" But his brothers could not answer him, so dismayed were they at his presence. Then Joseph said to his brothers, "Come closer to me." And they came closer. He said, "I am your brother, Joseph, whom you sold into Egypt. And now do not be distressed, or angry with yourselves, because you sold me here; for God sent me before you to preserve life. For the famine has been in the land these two years; and there are five more years in which there will be neither plowing nor harvest. God sent me before you to preserve for you a remnant on earth, and to keep alive for you many survivors. So it was not you who sent me here, but God; he has made me a father to Pharaoh, and lord of all his house and ruler over all the land of Egypt. Hurry and go up to my father and say to him, 'Thus says your son Joseph, God has made me lord of all Egypt; come down to me, do not delay. You shall settle in the land of Goshen, and you shall be near me, you and your children and your children's children, as well as your flocks, your herds, and all that you have. I will provide for you there—since there are five more years of famine to come so that you and your house-hold, and all that you have, will not come to poverty.' And now your eyes and the eyes of my brother Benjamin see that it is my own mouth that speaks to you. You must tell my father how great-ly I am honored in Egypt, and all that you have seen. Hurry and

bring my father down here." Then he fell upon his brother Ben-
jamin's neck and wept, while Benjamin wept upon his neck. And
he kissed all his brothers and wept upon them; and after that his
brothers talked with him.

Texts: **Genesis 45:3-15**
Psalm 37:1-11
Luke 6:27-38

O ur capacity to know and understand, to decode and ana-
lyze bewitches us. We imagine that we can see our life
whole and clear, and know how to act wisely. We think
we can do it in foreign policy, and we identify where our interests
are and make decisions. We can do it at work, for we know who
are our allies and our adversaries. We can even do it psychological-
ly, do enough therapy to see clearly and to act differently. Such a
capacity for clarity seduces us into being very sure. We end up
knowing exactly who we are and who God is and what God wants.
It makes us sure and often strident—frequently so sure as to be
destructive.

Into the midst of that clarity which gives us control, there is another reality that I announce to you, which is true, whether we like it or
not. It is this: There is something hidden, inscrutable, playful, and
unresolved about our human lives that warns us not to be too sure.
Such a claim is odd and uncomfortable for us, because it robs us of
deep certainty and ultimate control. We may say even more: That
hidden inscrutable, playful dimension of our life is an arena in
which the purposes of God may be at work among us in ways we

This sermon was preached at First Presbyterian Church, Dallas. The texts are
from the lectionary for the Seventh Sunday after the Epiphany.

do not even recognize. This hiddenness must be honored and taken seriously, because it is a way in which God does for us more than we can do for ourselves. The big word for this hidden power of God is providence. It means that God sees before (*pro-video*), that God knows well ahead of us and takes the lead in our lives. This is not the same as being "fated," or having our lives settled in the stars. It is rather a claim that God is a real power in our lives and is not simply a shadow or mirror of our own good intentions. God takes initiatives for our lives which may run counter to our own best intentions. Faithful people pay attention to this hiddenness and are willingly led by it.

In the Old Testament, the test case is Joseph in the book of Genesis. He was deeply resented by his older brothers because he was the family pet. In their resentment, the older brothers sold him off into slavery and pretended he had been killed. He ended up in Egypt. There, after being in prison for a time, he came to great power and influence in the Egyptian government. He turned out, after many years, to be the one who would give food to his needy, starving family. They received help from him, although they did not know who he was. When Joseph finally identified himself to his brothers, they did not recognize him right away. And then, when they recognized him, they were afraid. And with good reason, because he had a lot of unsettled grudges and angers to work out with them. He now had it in his power to banish them, or even to kill them, if he wanted to get even.

If Joseph's life had been only his private story that he could work out according to his loves and his hates, he would have been justified in killing his brothers, for he owed them a good bit of retaliation and getting even.

He does not do that, however, because he does not act out of his own, private inclination. On the face of it, his brothers had maltreated him, and he needed now belatedly to settle accounts. But Joseph, man of faith, takes a second hard look at his life. He is willing to host the hidden, inscrutable, unresolved purpose of God for his life that is beyond his control. He is willing to trust that there is a larger purpose being acted out in and through him, which he must honor and to which he must respond, even if it means denying his first raw inclination of anger and hate.

Thus, after he announces his name, "I am Joseph," he does two things. First, he gives assurance to his brothers that he is not going to kill them. He is not going to continue the vicious circle of fear and hate and violence that they had begun. He is willing to break the vicious circle and act in kindness toward his brothers. He is able to break the vicious circle only because he is willing to trust a purpose for his life that is larger than his own horizon.

Second, he tells his brothers exactly why he is willing to act in such a generous, unexpected way. He says it three times so they do not miss the point:

> God sent me before you to preserve life. (v. 5)
> God sent me before you to preserve for you a remnant. (v. 7)
> It was not you who sent me here, but God. (v. 8)

God sent, not you, not I, God sent. On that basis, Joseph embraces his brothers, gives them food, welcomes their father, gives them land, and permits them to begin a new life under his protection. He does a complete reversal from his deep resentment to an act of generosity, because he knows God has been at work well beyond him.

No doubt the brothers in their guilt must have thought, "No, we sent you here, because we hated you and we feared you." No doubt Joseph answered his brothers, "I thought that too. But then I became aware that a larger purpose was at work, transcending these petty quarrels, looking far into the future, and I became aware that my life was more than the sum of my little fears, my little hates, and my little loves. My life is larger than I imagined, and I decided to embrace that largeness that is God's gift for my life. I acted differently because I acted in ways befitting God's odd way with my life."

In his teaching in Luke 6, Jesus seems to take the Joseph narrative as a case in point. In the small, contained world where we live most of the time, we know whom to trust and whom to fear, whom to love and whom to hate. We get it all mapped out into good guys and bad guys, and everything is scheduled and predictable.

Jesus cuts through it all with four abrasive imperatives in vv. 27-28:

> Love your enemies.
> Do good to those who hate you.
> Bless those who curse you.
> Pray for those who abuse you.

Do what Joseph did. Jesus' teaching is not a scolding. And it is not a little romantic lesson in feeling good about everybody and acting silly. It is rather a rich, evangelical statement that there is more to life than our capacity to contain it all in our little moral categories, whereby life is reduced to a simple set of black/white, yes/no moral choices. For, says Jesus, if you reduce your life to the simple practice of loving your friends and hating your enemies, of being generous only to those you like and trust, and resistant whenever there is risk, what's the big deal? Anybody can do that. Any thief, any sinner, any atheist, any deal cutter, anybody who can count and remember and keep score can do that. But you, says Jesus to his disciples, are not part of that pitiful bunch of frightened people. You know more and you know differently, and you have freedom to act differently. You know about the large purposes of God, and you are called to act concretely as though the purposes of God really did make a difference in your life. For that is what it comes down to: Whether God is a real player in our lives, or whether we are in fact fearful, hate-filled atheists who must manage everything on our own, and who in fact love our fear and our anger and our hate and enjoy them a lot. It is wondrous, that right in the middle of all this talk about hate and love and enemies, Jesus speaks about the power of God:

- *Take another look* and consider "the Most High"
- *Take a second look,* and see that God is kind to the ungrateful and to the wicked
- *Take a painful second look,* and see that your Father is merciful, and be merciful

Act in the world as though the large purposes of God were operative. Then Jesus adds for his disciples three quick imperatives:

- Do not judge; you do not have to label and categorize everyone
- Forgive, and you will be forgiven
- Give, and it will be given to you

Do not judge . . . forgive . . . give. Forgive, give, share, yield, be generous—because God's powerful generosity moves through and over and in all our categories of control. Our faith invites us to be open to God's generosity, to receive it for ourselves and then for the others. And, like Joseph to his brothers, we break out of our tight, little control that makes us small, and petty, and fearful, and violent.

I am sure it crossed the mind of Joseph that if he was large-spirited, his brothers would take advantage of him. But then he reasoned, it does not matter, because God gives and intends more than the brothers can either give or withhold. In his trust, Joseph decided not to let the smallness of his brothers dictate the terms of his future.

These texts come up in the lectionary, and that is why they are before us here. But I will also tell you why I was glad to talk about them with you. There is something small and dangerous and greedy and brutal happening in our society that is meanspirited. We Christians who know about the merciful, generous God are the ones who must resist and counter that meanspiritedness which is so hateful and killing. I will cite three dimensions of that danger which you know very well:

- In terms of *religious morality*, it is scary that we are willing and able to sort people out like good potatoes and bad potatoes, and dismiss every one of whom we disapprove. We act as though we know fully, too fully, the mind of Christ. Such a neat little morality does not allow for the largeness of God's hidden way, which is more generous and more merciful than we can imagine.

- In terms of the *economy*, we are on our way to a more and more dangerous division of "haves" and "have-nots." We have lost most of our capacity for compassion in our society, and social care that has long been conventional in our history has become an ugly "liberal" idea. We are at the edge of concluding that poor people are wicked, undeserving people unloved by God, and we lucky ones must be God's chosen. And we construct our economic policies as though these" enemies" are of no positive interest to us. But these texts cut through our fearful habits, to assert that God's hidden generosity requires us to look again, so that we can escape these comfortable little categories which keep us slotted in hostility.

- In terms of *our families*, there is now an epidemic of stress on families. Old resentments surface, unresolved abuses linger—kids who don't act right, mates who behave badly, children that are unproductive embarrass us. Our families, like that of Joseph, become adversarial. The family becomes a powderkeg of hate and fear and resentment that too often ends in abuse, alienation, and violence. And now we, like Joseph, belatedly learn that the family is an area where God's power purposes redefine reality.

When we live according to our fears and our hates, our lives become small and defensive, lacking the deep, joyous generosity of God. If you find some part of your life where your daily round has grown thin and controlling and resentful, then these texts are for you. Life with God is much, much larger, shattering our little categories of control, permitting us to say that God's purposes led us well beyond ourselves to give and to forgive, to create life we would not have imagined.

This story of Joseph is an affirmation about providence. "Providence" is scary to "can-do" Americans. We fear we will lose free will and moral responsibility and all of that. But consider, it will not do to reduce life to our moral calculus, because we become grim and selfish and too sure, and then we die. The counterword on the lips of Joseph and in the life of Jesus in the very heart of the gospel is this:

You need not die. God has sent me to keep you alive.

The terms of life, however, are other than our own. They are the terms of the generous, merciful, giving, forgiving God. This God invites us to that new life, a second look, and a second life, forgiving, forgiven.

CHAPTER 3

I Will Do It . . .
But *You* Go

Exodus 3:1-12

*Moses was keeping the flock of his father-in-law Jethro, the priest of Midian; he led his flock beyond the wilderness, and came to Horeb, the mountain of God. There the angel of the L*ORD *appeared to him in a flame of fire out of a bush; he looked, and the bush was blazing, yet it was not consumed. Then Moses said, "I must turn aside and look at this great sight, and see why the bush is not burned up." When the L*ORD *saw that he had turned aside to see, God called to him out of the bush, "Moses, Moses!" And he said, "Here I am." Then he said, "Come no closer! Remove the sandals from your feet, for the place on which you are standing is holy ground." He said further, "I am the God of your father, the God of Abraham, the God of Isaac, and the God of Jacob." And Moses hid his face, for he was afraid to look at God.*

*Then the L*ORD *said, "I have observed the misery of my people who are in Egypt; I have heard their cry on account of their taskmasters. Indeed, I know their sufferings, and I have come down to deliver them from the Egyptians, and to bring them up out of that land to a good and broad land, a land flowing with milk and honey, to the country of the Canaanites, the Hittites, the Amorites, the Perizzites, the Hivites, and the Jebusites. The cry of the Israelites has now come to me; I have also seen how the Egyptians oppress them. So come, I will send you to Pharaoh to bring my people, the Israelites, out of Egypt." But Moses said to*

*God, "Who am I that I should go to Pharaoh, and bring the
Israelites out of Egypt?" He said, "I will be with you; and this
shall be the sign for you that it is I who sent you: when you have
brought the people out of Egypt, you shall worship God on this
mountain."*

Texts: Exodus 3:1-12
Psalm 103:1-13
Romans 8:18-15
Matthew 13:24-30, 36-43

oses was doing an ordinary thing, living an ordinary life,
herding ordinary sheep. Then there exploded in the
midst of his life the extraordinary, the miraculous. It
moved in against him, addressed him, summoned him, and his life
was changed irreversibly. The Bible does not quite know how to
talk about that intervention (as we do not know how to speak
about it), because the experience falls outside our usual way of talking. So the Bible speaks about a "bush burning," and an odd voice.

The real issue for Moses, however, is not the bush. What happened is that God came to confront Moses and to give him a large
purpose for his life that refused everything conventional. The reason we hold on to this old story and continue to ponder it is that
either we are people who have had this extraordinary reversal of
our life by God, so that nothing is ever the same again, or we wait
for and yearn for such a moment that will break our life open. We
hold this story because we know there is more to our life than the
ordinariness of life without the holiness of God.

The first thing that happens in this moment of extraordinary miracle is that God speaks. God announces for God's own self a very

*This sermon was preached at Spring Hill Presbyterian Church, Mobile, Alabama.
The texts are from the lectionary for the Seventh Sunday after Pentecost.*

specific identity. This is no generic God. It is rather the specific God of the book of Genesis:

> I am the God of your fathers, the God of Abraham, the God of
>   Isaac, the God of Jacob. (v. 6)

The statement might have added, "I am the God of Sarah, the God of Rebekah, the God of Rachel." I am the God of the old ancestral stories, the one who came upon hopeless old people and gave them children and new life, the one who came among wandering sojourners and promised them land, the one who came where life was all closed down and promised them a future they could not imagine or invent for themselves.

The first part of this story of Moses and the bush is a life-changing assertion: There are promises from God writ large in the faith of the church and in the life of the world. This story affirms (and we believe) that God has indeed made promises, and God will keep promises that run beyond all destructive hopelessness.

The alternative to promise is despair, which is what you get without the intrusion of this God. There are two kinds of people who despair. There are those who have nothing and who conclude they will never get anything. There are those, by contract, who have everything, and who want to keep it just the way it is. Both those who have nothing and those who have everything find promises impossible. Nonetheless, God's promises are rude and relentless. These promises do not honor our despair nor our complacency. We believe that God's future will cause a newness in the world, in which our old tired patterns of displacement and fear and hate cannot persist. In this "bush-narrative," God has come to enlist people into these promises for the future of Israel, and the future of the world.

Second, God speaks to Moses not only about the old promises and future expectations. God comes to speak also about God's immediate intention for the present tense:

> I have seen the misery of my people. . . . I have heard their cry on
> account of their taskmasters. I know their sufferings, and I have
> come down to deliver them from the hand of the Egyptians, and to
> bring them to a good land. . . . I have seen how the Egyptians
> oppress them. (vv. 7-9)

The God of the Bible takes notice of social suffering, in which some
are oppressed and others are oppressors, in which some are exploit-
ed and others are comfortable because of the exploitation. God
notices and God cares, and God acts decisively, because God will
not put up with these kinds of dysfunctional social arrangements.

There is presently a great quarrel in the North American church
about the nature of biblical faith and the God of the Bible. Is this
faith only about matters religious and pious and private, or is it
also about the great public questions of justice and equity in relation to economic and political reality? The argument is made differently here and there in the Bible. In this text, in any case, we are
at the core claim of biblical faith. The God of the Bible is pro-
foundly and perennially preoccupied with the kind of human suffering that comes when one brother or sister is able to establish
economic and political leverage over another brother or sister.
Because God is who God is, there must be liberation and transformation and the reestablishment of equity, a community in which
all attend to all.

In the epistle, from Romans 8, Paul, good Jew that he is, knows
about God's resolve for liberation. In an astonishing way, Paul
extends that resolve for liberation so that it concerns not just slaves
and peasants and nomads, but the whole of creation. Imagine the
whole of creation destined for an Exodus liberation!

> The creation waits with eager longing for the revealing of the chil-
> dren of God . . . [so] that the creation itself will be set free from its
> bondage to decay and will obtain the freedom of the glory of the
> children of God.
>
> (Rom. 8:19-21)

What a mouthful Paul wrote long before our environmental concerns! As Israel is enslaved to Pharaoh, so the creation is enslaved

to fear and anger and alienation, cursed under the distortion of the human community. And so creation cannot be fully liberated until true "children of God" appear, who can care for the earth differently. So says Paul, God wills the liberation of the world in order that the creation can be its fruitful, productive, and harmonious true self.

In these two speeches on the promises of Genesis (v. 6) and on the resolve of liberation (vv. 7-9), Moses is inducted by God into some of the largest and most definitional themes of biblical faith. Christians attest the promises of God, believing that the promises of God are at work in the world, unsettling every status quo and making the world new. We are people who celebrate God's resolve for liberation, in society and in creation, knowing that God wants us all to be liberated selves in a liberated creation. We affirm that the large forces of God's promise and God's resolve are at work, even though the world does not notice, and even though we ourselves do not always resonate with that work.

After the promises to Moses and the announcement of liberation to Moses, however, something very strange happens in the text of Exodus 3. In vv. 7-9, God has uttered a lot of first-person pronouns in which God takes initiative for what must come next: "I have seen, I know, I have come down to deliver, I have seen the oppression." God is deeply, directly, and personally involved in this crisis in Egypt and intends to do something about it. Upon hearing this speech of God, Moses must have thought, "This is indeed some impressive God—God is going to do all this, even though I do not know how it will all happen."

And then in v. 11, there is an odd, surprising turn in the rhetoric. The same God who has been uttering all these "I" statements now says to Moses:

So come, I will send you to Pharaoh to bring my people Israel out of Egypt. (v. 11)

"I will, I will, I will . . . so come, you go." What a turn-around. The trick is that all of these glorious things God has resolved to do are now abruptly assigned to Moses as human work. It is, moreover, dangerous human work. You be the liberator! You go to Pharaoh! You go to the big house and confront the entrenched, oppressive powers. You care enough to make the case for this bondaged people. What had been "I, I, I" now is suddenly "You, you, you."

What happens in one quick rhetorical flourish is that God's wondrous resolves are transposed into dangerous human work. That is how it often is in the Bible. God does God's work, to be sure; but the story of the Bible is the story of enlisting and recruiting human agents to do the things that God has promised. The book of Exodus is the tale of Moses' courageous life lived in defiance of Pharaoh for the sake of God's liberating resolve. Indeed, the resolve of God would not amount to much without the risky courage of Moses.

Now I assume that you are like Moses and like me—ordinary life, ordinary work, ordinary sheep to tend. Nonetheless, it does happen that the power of God explodes in our midst, and we get pushed out beyond our conventional horizon. It is, of course, possible to go on as though God's intrusion has not happened. Most of us, moreover, are timid and not inclined to crawl out very far on a limb. But it does happen, here and there, to people like us. And where it happens, the story moves to its next scene, for the story of this people is the story of folk who have agreed to do God's own work of promise and liberation.

I imagine, moreover, that the reason we need to think about this story of the bush and its unsettling invitation is that our society is in deep crisis. It is clear that most of our old patterns of life together are not working. This is indeed a time when the church may gather its faith together in order to think and pray and act differently. We are people who believe that God's old promises for well being and justice still persist in the world. We are people who believe that God's resolve for liberation in the world and of the world is a resolve of urgency that still pertains to the abused. And we are the ones who know that the promissory, liberating work of God devolves upon folk who do God's work in the world.

So Moses had his ordinariness broken. He had to rethink the faith and the life of his people. Moses discovered that his life was saturated with the reality of God. And some God this is! The Psalm for the day speaks of the God of the bush in this lyrical way:

> Who forgives all your iniquity,
>   who heals all your disease,
> who redeems your life from the Pit,
>   who crowns you with steadfast love and mercy,
> who satisfies you with good as long as you live,
>   so your youth is renewed like the eagle's,
> who works vindication and justice for all who are
>   oppressed.
>
> (Psalm 103:3-6)

And Moses wondered: What could be different about the purpose of my life because of the reality of this God?

4

The Midnight of Power and Weakness

Exodus 11:4-8; 12:29-32

Moses said, "Thus says the LORD: About midnight I will go out through Egypt. Every firstborn in the land of Egypt shall die, from the firstborn of Pharaoh who sits on his throne to the firstborn of the female slave who is behind the handmill, and all the firstborn of the livestock. Then there will be a loud cry throughout the whole land of Egypt, such as has never been or will ever be again. But not a dog shall growl at any of the Israelites—not at people, not at animals—so that you may know that the LORD makes a distinction between Egypt and Israel. Then all these officials of yours shall come down to me, and bow low to me, saying, 'Leave us, you and all the people who follow you.' After that I will leave." And in hot anger he left Pharaoh.

At midnight the LORD struck down all the firstborn in the land of Egypt, from the firstborn of Pharaoh who sat on his throne to the firstborn of the prisoner who was in the dungeon, and all the firstborn of the livestock. Pharaoh arose in the night, he and all his officials and all the Egyptians; and there was a loud cry in Egypt, for there was not a house without someone dead. Then he summoned Moses and Aaron in the night, and said, "Rise up, go away from my people, both you and the Israelites! Go, worship the LORD, as you said. Take your flocks and your herds, as you said, and be gone. And bring a blessing on me too!"

Texts: Exodus 11:4-8, 12:29-32
Mark 15:33-39
1 Corinthians 1:27-31

These verses in Exodus are the culmination of our model story of faith and freedom. The encounter that is reported is a savagely unequal one. On the one hand, there is feeble Israel, pitiful slaves, led by Moses. In the older stories of Genesis, from Abraham to Joseph, this people had been given a blessing by God, a power for life that it carried in its midst from generation to generation. All through the book of Genesis, we can see the Israelites bestowing their special blessing on all sorts of people. By the time of our narrative in the book of Exodus, however, that life-force given by God has been completely submerged and robbed of its vitality. Israel has been reduced to nothing more than a pitiful band of helpless slaves, without any clout and without enough significance even to be noticed in the empire.

On the other hand, there is Pharaoh, mighty Egypt, the dominant superpower, the neighborhood bully used to having his own way. All through the Exodus narrative, Pharaoh in his bluster has been in control, endlessly posturing, threatening, exploiting, intimidating, using and abusing, and Israel has been helplessly on the receiving end. Israel had hoped to escape, but Pharaoh is determined not to lose his supply of cheap labor.

Thus the relative power of each part is clear and unambiguous. Pharaoh will dominate; Israel will submit. In chapter 11, however, Moses makes an incredible assertion that reverses the flow of conventional power. Moses announces to Pharaoh that at midnight, in the darkness, in the hiddenness of the night, Yahweh—the untamed factor in the imperial process, the undomesticated character in the story of Israel—will make a devastating entry into the drama. In the darkness of midnight, so that no one will see, Yah-

---

This sermon was preached during summer school at Columbia Theological Seminary.

The Midnight of Power and Weakness   25

weh will come against the empire, killing and destroying all the firstborn, causing the empire to cry in deep grief and dismay. And all the while, Israel will be asleep in its vulnerable slave huts, will remain unscathed, untouched, and undisturbed. That is what Yahweh will do, the God whom Pharaoh has dismissed as irrelevant.

In chapter 12, events occurred just as Moses announced in chapter 11. At midnight, just when no one could see, the Lord struck down the firstborn of the empire, while Israel slept away peacefully. At midnight the inexplicable force of God's holiness intruded into the struggle. The force that arrived at midnight is beyond both the understanding and the control of Pharaoh. It is beyond the expectation of Israel as well. At midnight Yahweh struck down all the firstborn of the empire, all the beloved of this haughty regime. There was such a loud cry of dismay and grief, louder than that of abused slaves, louder than anyone in the big house had ever cried before, because kings do not publicly process their pain.

The moment of death in the darkness was a big lesson for Pharaoh. He learned in an instant what he had massively resisted and refused to learn. He learned that he was not in control, and that he had in Yahweh met more than his match. He learned that there is a deep, hidden resolve loosed in the empire that works on behalf of the abused, seemingly powerless slaves. He learned of his own helplessness before God's power for life. In the twinkling of an eye, Pharaoh undertakes a complete reversal of imperial policy. Pharaoh had worked hard to keep the slaves from escaping, in order to preserve his work force. Now Pharaoh issues new, unexpected imperatives to this slave company: "Rise, go, go worship, take your flocks and your herds as you said, and be gone." Pharaoh had valued these slaves for his own purposes, but now their value has turned to deep threat. Finally, even Pharaoh can come to see that trying to hold God's beloved in bondage is futile, costly, and counterproductive. At midnight Pharaoh is able to see the surge of life to which he has no access.

In this awesome reversal of imperial policy, there is Pharaoh's series of imperatives that concedes everything. Then Pharaoh issues one more stunning imperative, one of the most astonishing utterances in all of human history. After Moses had for so long addressed truth to power, now finally, pitifully, power speaks to truth. Pharaoh feebly says to departing Moses, "Bless me, be a blessing to me, bless me as well."

What an utterance! In this utterance, all of worldly power is gathered in a moment of honest vulnerability, presenting itself in its acknowledged need, presenting itself helplessly to the throne of weakness and insignificance. This utterance by Pharaoh to Moses anticipates David before Nathan, Zedekiah before Jeremiah, Pilate before Jesus, Agrippa before Paul, Charles V before Luther, Hitler before Niemoeller, DeKlerk before Mandela, Wallace before King, Reagan before Wiesel, Husack before Havel. This is power before weakness—not just any weakness, but the weakness perceived to be a carrier of God's new possibility for the earth, in the very midst of the shambles of arrogance and pride and violence. And the perception comes just at midnight.

In this moment, this nobody of a people, Moses' people Israel, is seen, even by the rulers of this age, to be a carrier of God's future in the world, a large possibility that Pharaoh himself now knows that he himself cannot sponsor or bring to fruition. Who would have thought that down in the slave huts there reside all the promises of God, until this Pharaoh who seems to have everything his way comes at midnight, hat in hand, and says in a massively embarrassed petition, "Bless me, give me life, do for me what I cannot do for myself." In that moment all power in the world is reordered and life surges with new possibility, because the surge of blessing that God has long ago lodged with this people is now made public and visible.

As you hear this narrative and are present to Pharaoh's astonishing midnight acknowledgment, you may enter the narrative as you choose, even in more than one role:

- You might, if you choose, be the small, weak underling who turns out to be a carrier of powerful blessing that only waits to be recognized. I submit that the church may be just such a carrier of blessing in consumer America, which Pharaoh will have to face.

- You might be for a while the large dominant power who is used to having it all your own way, with an awareness of your own impressive influence. But now in a moment of terribly anguished recognition and self-awareness, you sense that God's gift of life is not in your possession. The power of blessing is outside you, and you must receive it from some of those whom you have bullied.

- Or you might take the entire drama inside your body, there to discover that your secret gift of life from God is found in the very parts of your body and your person which remain unnoticed and unrealized. You must, perforce, turn the strong effective parts of your self to the dismissed parts, in order to receive your future where you least expected it. And you must do it at midnight.

This text is about the shattering of all old maps of power and control, the exposure of all assumptions of power and weakness that are mistaken. We may now discover that God has located the seeds of new life just where we would never think to look for them. In the Christian tradition we dare say that the blessing of God is located in the life of Jesus, whose life is bracketed in powerlessness between Herod at the beginning and Pilate at the end. But the whole world turns to him like the final centurion and says, "Bless me."

The drama of blessing, so poignant in Jesus, is not confined to the body of Jesus. It is also at work, according to God's odd calculus, where the failed, emptied forms of power must come in petition to the hidden, unnoticed carriers of life. It is such a scandal, but then our faith is built on the scandalous affirmation that the power of God is given in hiddenness, so that more blatant forms of power must come and finally, just after midnight, say "Bless me."

The story of Pharaoh is the story of failed power; the story of Moses is about unnoticed but irresistible possibility. The story is played out, just after midnight.

Listen to this from 1 Corinthians 1:27-31:

> But God chose what is foolish in the world to shame the wise; God chose what is weak in the world to shame the strong; God chose what is low and despised in the world, things that are not, to reduce to nothing things that are, so that no one might boast in the presence of God. He is the source of your life in Christ Jesus, who became for us wisdom from God, and righteousness, and sanctification and redemption, in order that, as it is written, "Let the one who boasts, boast in the Lord."

5

Wondrous Solidarity, Devastating Starchiness

Exodus 33:18—34:10

Moses said, "Show me your glory, I pray." And [the Lord] said, "I will make all my goodness pass before you, and will proclaim before you the name, 'The Lord'; and I will be gracious to whom I will be gracious, and will show mercy on whom I will show mercy. But," he said, "you cannot see my face; for no one shall see me and live." And the Lord continued, "See, there is a place by me where you shall stand on the rock; and while my glory passes by I will put you in a cleft of the rock, and I will cover you with my hand until I have passed by; then I will take away my hand, and you shall see my back; but my face shall not be seen."

The Lord said to Moses, "Cut two tablets of stone like the former ones, and I will write on the tablets the words that were on the former tablets, which you broke. Be ready in the morning, and come up in the morning to Mount Sinai and present yourself there to me, on the top of the mountain. No one shall come up with you, and do not let anyone be seen throughout all the mountain; and do not let flocks or herds graze in front of that mountain." So Moses cut two tablets of stone like the former ones; and he rose early in the morning and went up on Mount Sinai, as the Lord had commanded him, and took in his hand the two tablets of stone. The Lord descended in the cloud and stood with him there, and proclaimed the name, "The Lord." The Lord passed before him, and proclaimed,

"The LORD, the LORD,
a God merciful and gracious,
slow to anger,
and abounding in steadfast love and faithfulness,
keeping steadfast love for the thousandth generation,
forgiving iniquity and transgression and sin,
yet by no means clearing the guilty,
but visiting the iniquity of the parents
upon the children
and the children's children,
to the third and the fourth generation."

And Moses quickly bowed his head toward the earth, and worship-
ed. He said, "If now I have found favor in your sight, O LORD, I
pray, let the LORD go with us. Although this is a stiff-necked people,
pardon our iniquity and our sin, and take us for your inheritance."

He said: I hereby make a covenant. Before all your people I
will perform marvels, such as have not been performed in all the
earth or in any nation; and all the people among whom you live
shall see the work of the LORD; for it is an awesome thing that I
will do with you.

Texts: Exodus 33:18–34:10
Luke 23:32-38

Moses turned out to be almost as tough a customer as Yahweh. The covenant at Sinai had just been violated in the orgy of the golden calf (Exod. 32:1-6), and Yahweh has responded in murderous rage (Exod. 32:35). One might expect Moses to grovel and petition in ingratiating deference. Instead,

This sermon was preached in the Graduate Theological Union, Berkeley, on the
occasion of the inauguration of Glenn Bucher, erstwhile Dean at Columbia Theo-
logical Seminary, as the President of the GTU. The larger theme for the events
surrounding the inauguration was the way in which religion is both a resource for
and an impediment to peaceable human pluralism.

Wondrous Solidarity, Devastating Starchiness   31

however, Moses does hard-nosed bargaining with God (Exod. 33:12-16). He almost gets his way with God, even after God's rage. Moses says, in a last, insistent demand, "Show me your glory" (Exod. 33:18).

But Yahweh will not let Moses go that far, or see that far into the very mystery of God. God answers Moses and says: You can see my back but not my face.

> There is a place by me where you shall stand up on the rock; and while my glory passes by I will put you in a cleft of the rock, and I will cover you with my hand until I have passed by; then I will take away my hand and you will see my back; but my face will not be seen.
>
> (Exod. 33:21-23)

Moses is to watch . . . and God will "moon" him!

> And so, says the narrator, it happened that way:
> The Lord descended in the cloud and stood with him there, and proclaimed the name "The Lord." The Lord passed before him.
> (34:5)

Characteristically, the Bible pays no attention to the mooning or to God's back side, or to what Moses saw. It focuses instead (it always does) upon what God said and what Moses heard.

This is what God said to Moses in this awesome moment of self-disclosure, when God became palpable in the present of Moses:

> The Lord, the Lord,
> a God merciful and gracious,
> slow to anger,
> and abounding in steadfast love and faithfulness,
> keeping steadfast love for the thousandth generation,
> forgiving iniquity and transgression and sin.
> (34:6-7a)

What a mouthful! Here is the sum of evangelical faith. Here is the substance of a radical theology of grace. Here is the primal warrant in the Bible for the claim that at its core, reality is concerned with healing, reconciliation, forgiveness, and, finally, inclusiveness.

All the great words of Israel's faith occur here, all the words that we Christians claim we have seen embodied in Jesus of Nazareth. In a rough but adequate way, all these words are synonyms: merciful, gracious, steadfast love (twice), faithfulness, forgiveness. If one is to learn Hebrew for theological purposes, begin with this set of words. God is for us. God is for us all. God wants this relation to work with Israel, indeed with the world. This is the voice of Israel's liberator and the world's creator. Here we see what is most wondrous and odd, distinctive and unique about the God of the Bible.

These words do indeed tell the truth about God, the truth that has been so about God before the beginning of time, the truth that drives the gospel, the truth about God . . . and therefore the truth about humanity, and therefore the truth about us. Life consists in "yes" from God (see 2 Cor. 1:19) that is not negated even by the orgies of recalcitrance and autonomy and greed and brutality to which we are daily tempted. The "yes" of God's gospel matters decisively for the life of the world. And here it is given, in detail, one word at a time, to Moses who must have watched and heard while he was utterly stunned. Indeed, we are stunned, if we watch and listen carefully.

Note well: Yahweh did not stop this wondrous self-disclosing speech on such a happy note, with such a marvelous statement of solidarity with Moses and with Israel. Yahweh continues this decisive self-revelation:

> Yet [who will] by no means clear the guilty,
> but visiting the iniquity of the parents upon the children
> and the children's children,
> to the third and the fourth generation.
>
> (34:7b)

This second half of Yahweh's self-identity is not only a mouthful, it is a heavy-duty, ominous conversation-stopper. Things must have gotten very quiet for Moses on the mountain in that moment of utterance. It had just been grace upon grace. But now Yahweh has reversed field. The God who had spoken in such wondrous solidarity now speaks in a new, unaccommodating tone.

Such strange and hard words—guilty, iniquity—and with longevity for four generations, a long time to answer for sin. This speech of Yahweh introduces severe starchiness into the conversation. There are rules and laws and commands and expectations that persist through time, all watched over by this uncompromising sovereign. The creation is not endlessly supple for our whims and desires, and the program at Sinai is not (as we say) indeterminate. There is a shape and intention. And Yahweh will not be mocked!

The core theological problem for Moses, and left from Moses for all of us, is how to hold all of this together. I have pondered this long, and it boils down finally to a deep contradiction. Oh, I know, even the promises are conditional and not free-form. There are ways to weasel through the contradiction. But finally, it is a contradiction. When God thinks about Israel's well-being, there is forgiveness. But when God thinks about God and being God as God does, there will be no mocking.

God for us/God for God's self . . . a systematics may harmonize it all. But at the raw level of utterance, it is like one's love for a teenager in the family which on occasion is driven out by impatience and rage that will erupt beyond the yearning of love. I wonder whether Yahweh noticed the contradiction in God's own utterance. Or perhaps God never thinks in terms of divine perfectibility but is content to be a Jewish God filled with contradictions and disjunctions that are proper to Jewishness with all its candor and its courage and its hopefulness. Perhaps Yahweh did not notice. But in this overflow of self-giving to Moses at the mountain, God let it all surface, for all of it belongs to God.

But Moses noticed the problem, even if God did not. Moses noticed that plan A, the statement of graciousness in vv. 6-7a, would be marvelous. But plan B (v.7b) of hard accountability is exceedingly tough. If you act that way, O Lord, who should stand?

For all the contradiction in the statement, this utterance is the very truth of the God of the Bible. This very God who gracefully embraces is the Lord of unutterable and uncompromising demand. It is the very truth of God. All of our self-hatred cannot eradicate God's generosity; and all our warm, fuzzy positiveness cannot override the reality that God will be God, with all the inexplicable rights and privileges pertaining thereto—and we do not have to like it.

That is how the rule of this God is ordered, ordered in awesome self-giving and ordered in a savage self-serving by the God who will not be mocked. I know of course the programmatic arguments that grace wins out—except that none of us imagines that in the end we live in a morally indifferent or ethically incoherent world. We would not be about this faith business unless we believed that God's terrible way is beyond us. We cannot cope by projecting something other, when we know that God's awesome untamedness is out there *for us* and *against us*. This word from God is not about patriarchalism or any of those matters to which we object, but it is the recognition that holiness from God lives at the very core of reality and will not be framed or tamed for our preferred world.

Moreover, this deep unsettledness comes to the earth. It must come to earth and it does so in hard and dangerous ways. There are those among us who are touched by the graciousness of God and find in that touch a warrant for caring inclusiveness. There are also those among us who take up the wild severity of God and read from it an agenda of demanding, impatient moral distinctiveness. It can hardly be otherwise, if we think this whole text is true and if we insist that heaven does come to earth. For when heaven comes to earth what we get is not only the wondrous solidarity of forgiveness but also the starchiness of God's holiness. The program of severity is difficult for us to bear, because it does spin off into intolerant human claims, with just enough warrant to make it as dangerous and compelling as God's own claim.

We will, inevitably, given who we are—our urbaneness, our afflu-ence, our discrete tolerance, our embrace of gospel graciousness—do our best to overcome and cancel out the severity on earth, and do our best in our theology to read it away from heaven as well. We prefer to handle this deep trouble by taking the first half of Yah-weh's speech as the whole speech, and imagining that God stopped the self-disclosure at v. 7a, before the severe part was spoken.

I suggest, however, that Moses and the biblical text generally take a very different strategy in coping with this word from Yahweh. The Bible does not seek to explain away the tough utterance of God, but with enormous, passionate courage, Moses and his ilk wade into God's dilemma and seek to leverage God.

Thus Moses, upon hearing this terrible contradiction of gra-ciousness and heavy visitation (or, as we say, inclusiveness and dis-tancing sovereignty), quickly bowed his head toward the earth and worshiped (Exod. 34:9). He bowed before the contradiction in God's very life. He worshiped the God of grace and of hard visita-tion, the wholeness of God in all of God's unresolve. And then he prayed. In his prayer he walked into the center of God's unresolve, and committed an overt act of advocacy, urging God this time round to exercise option A and not option B. He says,

> If now, I have found favor in your sight, O Lord, I pray, let the Lord go with us. Although this is a stiff-necked people, pardon our iniq-uity and our sin, and take us for your inheritance.
>
> (34:9)

Be the God of graciousness and do not savage us with plan B. The advocacy of Moses, commented with hutzpah and at considerable risk, makes the case for Israel.

Yahweh answers, for this time with the implementation of plan A, growing out of the utterance of plan A:

> I hereby make a covenant. Before all the peoples I will perform miracles such as have not been performed in all the earth or in any nation. . . . It is an awesome thing I will do with you. (34:10)

And so the fragile history of Israel begins again, this time once again with plan A, without which Israel has no future.

Our own work is no different, I submit, from the work of Moses. It is proper that at the beginning of President Bucher's leadership, this company should take stock of its situation and its proper vocation out of this dangerous text. I understand that the Union wants to be intellectually credible and careful, urbane and well-thought-of. But the truth is that all of us, including this Union, are now poised at a dangerous place midst the unresolve of God that flows off as unresolve into the real world around us.

We are rightly vexed about religion as a source of healing inclusiveness and religion as a source of hateful destructiveness. We should not, however, breeze the problem away as liberals, as though it were really a psychological disorder or a sociological mistake. The vexation we now face is rooted in God's own life, and has been visible since Moses at Sinai, and now permeates the courts of heaven as it does the corridors of earth.

The theological task, given this unresolved state of God, is not simply judicious believing and detached adjudication. It is rather advocacy born of Moses' hutzpah, to storm into the very core of God's life and insist that God's truth as healing is a profound claim in the face of God's well-discerned severity. So our work, as intellectuals and as citizens of this unresolved time, is as the advocacy of Moses,

- *priests* who petition for plan A,
- *rabbis* who instruct God in plan A,
- *thinkers and actors* who carry the advocacy—intellectual, polical, cultural, artistic—from heaven, where it is rooted, into the burdens and anguishes of the earth, where healing seems always defeated in the face of severity.

It is telling and astonishing that, according to Luke (albeit with a textual problem), as Jesus came to be crucified as the enemy of his government and of his church and (some thought) of his people, he prayed. He did not instruct or even act as an advocate on earth, but he petitioned the God who was at a loss that day.

> Father, forgive them, for they know not what they do.
> (Luke 23:34)

The prayer suggests that on that Friday, matters could have gone either way. God could have responded to the crisis by the severity of Exod. 34:7b, to the third and fourth generation. It was not predetermined that Friday would be a day of salvation. It could have been a day of God's crushing, retaliating severity. But Jesus, like Moses, makes a powerful bid for plan A. And we have confessed since then that it was made into a day of grace-filled conciliation.

The prayer of Jesus and the advocacy of Moses must always be done over again because the issues before this great Jewish God and before the Union are of the same kind. So while exercised by the dilemma of religion as healing and religion as hate, we cannot lightly pretend the harshness of heaven away. This Union could be a place where advocacy is undertaken—intellectually, politically, artistically, liturgically—toward heaven and on earth, not wishing, but risking, entering the lists on the side of plan A, not neutral and objective and detached, but alive to the issues where heaven and earth struggle for the truth of God. Such an enterprise would be a break with much academic security. In a new epistemological situation, plan A matters now, as it did at Sinai and at Calvary.

PART

TWO

Prophetic Texts

CHAPTER 6

Power for Life Flown in by a Bird

1 Kings 17:17-24

After this the son of the woman, the mistress of the house, became ill; his illness was so severe that there was no breath left in him. She then said to Elijah, "What have you against me, O man of God? You have come to me to bring my sin to remembrance, and to cause the death of my son!" But he said to her, "Give me your son." He took him from her bosom, carried him up into the upper chamber where he was lodging, and laid him on his own bed. He cried out to the LORD, "O LORD my God, have you brought calamity even upon the widow with whom I am staying, by killing her son?" Then he stretched himself upon the child three times, and cried out to the LORD, "O LORD my God, let this child's life come into him again." The LORD listened to the voice of Elijah; the life of the child came into him again, and he revived. Elijah took the child, brought him down from the upper chamber into the house, and gave him to his mother; then Elijah said, "See, your son is alive." So the woman said to Elijah, "Now I know that you are a man of God, and that the word of the LORD in your mouth is truth."

Texts: 1 Kings 17:17-24
Mark 5:35-43

The trouble in Israel was structural and systemic. There was no rain. The drought brought with it death. Drought is an ancient form of energy crisis. The energy crisis means that the government has failed. The king could not cause rain, could not give life. The king was impotent, the government was discredited. The world had failed. The situation was right for despair and dismay.

Such an energy crisis affected everyone, rich and poor. As usual, however, the crisis impinged upon the poor first, and most decisively. Our attention is focused on a nameless woman. Such women are always nameless. She had nothing, neither name nor food nor hope. Actually, she had one thing, her beloved son. He was her only hope, her welfare system, her lean link to life.

The story begins in the failed royal system with this nameless, forelorn widow. Elijah enters the story. He is another kind of character. He is uncredentialed, uncontaminated by the system, uncompromised by government plans for rain. He is also untested, because nobody knows what he can do. He works through no royal arrangements. He is simply dispatched by Yahweh, an abrupt, unexplained command: "Go to the widow" (v. 9). He goes. He goes to meet the widow. Oddly, he gives her an unending supply of food (v. 16). He does for her what the king cannot do.

The plot now thickens and we pick up the story. Elijah did the wondrous miracle of food, solving the hunger crisis. Now, however, the stakes are much higher. The boy, the widow's only hope in this age or in the age to come, dies (v. 17). She loses her son. She loses her grip on reality. She loses her cool. She blames Elijah for his death: "Why have you come against me—to cause the death of my

This sermon was preached on Ash Wednesday in the Columbia Theological Seminary chapel. The readings were selected for the occasion.

son!" (v. 18). She is frightened, perhaps embarrassed that she trusted such an odd man. She panics, because she has lost her life support and has now entered her personal energy crisis. Probably she is a little guilty that she mistrusted the royal system. There is a death. Someone must be blamed. She draws the conclusion that if you deal with this man, trouble will come. (That is the same conclusion drawn by the king, 18:17.)

The death of the boy looms more severe than drought or hunger. We watch to see what this odd man will do now. Nobody would expect a king to deal with death, as kings never claim power for such ultimate matters. Elijah, however, has hinted at much more than any king would undertake. Could Elijah now do what kings won't try to do?

He is abrupt, magisterial, not caught in the woman's terror. He acts decisively: "Give me your son" (v. 19). He takes the boy into his care and into his power. He gives the impression to the widow that he is prepared to take on even the reality of death. He is prepared to take on the deep problem the king will not address. He is prepared to do what the king cannot do.

Elijah acts in a remarkable way. He prays. He turns the problem of death over to the reality of God. He speaks to make death be a concern for God. His words open the problem of death to the power and care of God. The woman is not now in the scene. There is only Elijah. He dominates the action and the drama. Elijah prays twice. His prayer asserts that the reality of death is a larger issue than this woman ever suspected. The limits and edges of life concern the reality, power, and faithfulness of God. Elijah knew that.

Elijah's first prayer is an accusation against God (v. 20). Elijah knows that God deals in matters of life and death. Elijah asks God if God has caused this death, for Elijah knows that he himself is not responsible. There is of course no answer from God, as God will not take such bait. Elijah at prayer, however, is determined, powerful, and filled with authority. He prays again. This time he prays an imperative to God. His is a voice of deep, demanding faith. Elijah speaks to God in an imperative: "Return the life of this child" (v. 21). God holds the power for life. Some may have thought the king was in charge of life, but the king does not figure in the world of Elijah. Elijah has recast the human issue and there is only death, God, and prayer.

God yields to Elijah. Elijah has compelled God to act. God heard (v. 22)! (God *shema'd*.) God gives life back to the boy at the behest of Elijah. The boy lives (v. 22)! The prayer, faith, courage, and daring of Elijah have changed the world. Elijah takes the new-birthed boy back to the mother, who is frantic, confused, and upset. Elijah says simply, "Your son lives" (v. 23). Elijah does not celebrate himself. He does not even mention God nor bear witness to God. He only describes the new reality wrought out of intense, demanding faith.

The woman is as changed as the boy. The last time she had spoken, she had accused Elijah (v. 18). But now she celebrates Elijah without reservation: "I know you are a man of God. The word of God is in your mouth" (v. 24). The woman knows that where new life comes, the unexpected power of God is visible. She celebrates Elijah, but she confesses much more: I know God has not quit. I know the power for life is at work. I know the rule of God is not contained in the pitiful little regime of the pitiful, dysfunctional king. Indeed, the king is completely absent from this drama. Why would anyone call on him? He can do nothing. Life has broken loose; the king cannot enact life; the king cannot block life from coming. "My son was dead and is alive!" God has done what the king cannot do.

This is a story about the oddness of Elijah. Elijah is shown to have the power for life. That power is not explained; it is only witnessed to. It is linked to faith and to prayer, to a refusal to accept the widow's little faith or the king's little power. The world enacted by Elijah breaks all such conventions, routines, and stereotypes: New news has come. The boy lives! The news given us in this story is that the power for life is offered. It is carried by a human agent.

This is Lent. We are in a season on the way to new life, but now it is time for passion, suffering, death, denial, repentance. In our Lent we yearn for Easter. In our deathliness, we wonder about the gift of life. Our question is the same question asked by Elijah and the widowed mother. It is the question of life. How is life possible among us in our massive, resistant defeats? How is life possible?

The text gives us a cue, but no explanation. Earlier in this same chapter, Elijah is called and commissioned by Yahweh, called in the midst of the drought to deal with the energy crisis (v. 1). Elijah is sent by God to drink from the brook and to eat the food given to him by ravens (v. 4). The food he is offered is not very tasty food, for it tastes like the dribble of birds. It is not very reliable food, not as reliable as the king's sumptuous table. Elijah had to depend on the flight of the ravens. It turned out, nonetheless, to be adequate food. Morning and evening, bread and meat, the birds kept the air-lift going. Elijah had water and enough to eat. (v. 6).

His food supply seems tenuous, but God gives him enough. His food supply lies outside the administration of the king. His is not a government grant. Elijah is cut off from the luxury and certitude of the king, but he is also free from royal junk food. He does not obey the king. He does not participate in the energy crisis which is the king's special problem. Understand, he does not fight the king either. He simply proceeds with the assurance that the king is fundamentally irrelevant to the basic human issues of food, health, justice, and life. I submit that Elijah's willingness to eat what the ravens flew in is what gave him energy and courage and freedom and authority. He had energy with the woman, courage in the face of death, authority in the practice of prayer.

Two things come clear in this story about Lent.

First, the power for life in the face of our deathliness is urgent. We are surrounded by fallen sons and hopeless widows. We yearn to have that power to transform life.

Second, that power for life is probably not available when we eat too well in the presence of the king. Elijah's power comes along with his eating habits.

Lent is a time to think about another diet, another nourishment, another loyalty. In various ways, we are all seduced, domesticated, and bought off—economically, religiously, intellectually, political-ly, morally. It is the story of our life. Bought-off people never have power for life. That is what makes the Elijah narrative so compelling and dangerous for us. It is another story about another power, based in another diet.

The Lenten agenda for us all is this: Is it possible to do what the king cannot do? Life is indeed offered. But it is not given cheaply or at random. It is not given the way the world would dispense such power. No wonder the woman was amazed. Life has to do with sons given back, with daughters restored, with energy and courage granted, with hope and joy and well-being made new for us. Life is promised to the ones who eat thin and pray hard. Life is given by God. Power is granted to do what the king can never do.

7

Afterward . . .
After George . . .
After Bill . . . Newness

Isaiah 1:21-27

How the faithful city has become a whore!
    She that was full of justice,
righteousness lodged in her—
    but now murderers!
Your silver has become dross,
    your wine is mixed with water.
Your princes are rebels and companions of thieves.
Everyone loves a bribe and runs after gifts.
They do not defend the orphan,
and the widow's cause does not come before them.
Therefore says the Sovereign, the Lord of hosts,
    the Mighty One of Israel:
Ah, I will pour out my wrath on my enemies,
    and avenge myself on my foes!
I will turn my hand against you;
I will smelt away your dross as with lye
    and remove all your alloy.
And I will restore your judges as at the first,
    and your counselors as at the beginning.
Afterward you shall be called the city of righteousness,
    the faithful city.
Zion shall be redeemed by justice,
    and those in her who repent, by righteousness.

Texts: Isaiah 1:21-27
Hebrews 11:8-16
Luke 19:41-44

They would not let me delay my sermon title until after the election. I therefore had to include both the president and the governor (alternatively, the president and the president-elect), knowing of course that we would indeed be "after" one of them. My assigned topic in this series is the urban crisis and the prospect of the city. It is the prophet Isaiah, more than anyone else in the Bible, who thinks relentlessly about the city. To be sure, the city about which he thinks is not New Haven or Barcelona or Atlanta or Rio de Janeiro or Johannesburg, or any of our contemporary candidates. He thinks always about the city of Jerusalem, that ancient media center, financial center, symbolic center of all reality, practical center of all power. And when we think of other cities, we imagine all our other cities that function not unlike Jerusalem, center of possibility and engine for brutality.

At the outset of the book of Isaiah, there is this poem in 1:21-27 which anticipates the whole of the long book of Isaiah. That poem lays down the themes for the history of the city which Isaiah will narrate, concerning the next two hundred years. I have taken up this text, because I suggest that Isaiah gives the long-term story of every major city, and not only Jerusalem. Viewed theologically, every city behaves and has a story to tell like that of Jerusalem, laden with power for life and death. So take the poem and with it reimagine your favorite city, even this city.

This sermon was preached at the United Church on the Green in New Haven, Connecticut. It was part of a series of sermons that summer and fall on the urban crisis as it concerns the church. It was preached on November 8, 1992, the Sunday after the election of President Clinton. It had to be written before the election, however, and I therefore kept my options open.

The poem begins by plunging us into *an honest notice of the mess in the city*. As poets are wont to do, Isaiah uses the language of marital, covenantal fidelity to characterize the city. The city was begun as a noble, humane operation with an intentional, honorable, peaceable identity. And then it was all thrown over for more immediate, lascivious achievements.

> How the faithful city has become a whore. (v. 21)

Once so faithful, now so fickle; once so committed, now so self-gratifying. The lady has become a tramp or, to move past the sexism of the image, the gentleman has become a paramour, seeking satiation and disregarding the well-being of all others. The poet offers a stark contrast between what once was and what is now—was full of justice, now murderers; was full of righteousness, now brutality.

Life has become cheap, careless, compromised; silver becomes waste ore, wine cheapened with water. Nothing is as good as it seems, and justice is as watered down as the wine. The word, the coin, the institutions, the policies, are all contaminated by self-interest, all trivialized for quick, dishonest gain.

The corruption and distortion were really symptoms of a trickle-down system. It started at the top so it is not a bad theme for post-election Sunday. Princes, people in power, rebels, violating order to be on the make; everyone loves a bribe, pursues gifts, takes payoffs.

We began with a sexual metaphor and moved to economic components, and now we come to the inevitable, quite visible conclusion:

> They do not defend the orphan,
> and the widow's cause does not come before them. (v. 23)

Widows and orphans in that ancient, patriarchal society are the ones who have lost their male advocates and breadwinners, and who therefore are completely vulnerable and sure to be destitute. The tramp-city, now the scene of payoffs and deals and unbridled self-interest, no longer has in its purview the justice and righteousness and guarantees of well-being for its most vulnerable members.

Thus is Jerusalem, so the present-tense verbs; there is something about the city that forgets the very mandate of fidelity that makes a city work. There is nothing here about removing these failed poor and making them invisible, deporting them because they are an economic inconvenience. No, because widows and orphans are not an inconvenience. They are a measure of the health of the city, to be measured in terms of justice and righteousness, and Jerusalem has failed that measure, because of unbridled self-interest that does careless damage to the powerless.

The outcome: You did not think, did you, that this city (holy as it is) or any city, would make this move to injustice unscathed? The poet Isaiah moves dramatically to a second major accent. *Therefore* . . . as a result. From the truth about the city comes this terrible consequence. It follows in the long run story of the city:

> *Therefore*, says the Sovereign . . .
> *Therefore* God . . .
> *Therefore* the holy purpose of God intrudes upon the city
> that thought itself immune and autonomous and free to
> order its own life.

In a quick piece of rhetoric, the city that thought it was on its own, is drawn into the circle of this awful, uncompromising sovereign. One can make that connection only with poetry that brings odd things together. This poetry brings together in one breath the city and the sovereign, and now we ponder that terrible connection.

"Therefore," says the God who seemed to be driven out of urban planning long since. But, says the poetry, there is a subtext in every urban situation, for the holy one is the final guarantor and judge of the city.

> Therefore, I will pour out my wrath,
> I will avenge myself,

> I will turn my hand against you,
> I will smelt away your dross as with lye,
> I will remove all your alloy,
> I will restore your early judges.
>
> (vv. 24-26)

The city, beyond its own choices, is caught up in the terrible calculus of God's rule that will not be mocked. You see, the city is not just a political engine or an economic cluster; it is a theological entity that in the end must face its God-shaped destiny, a destiny it cannot evade nor avoid.

The whoring city that can no longer remember its character of fidelity to its vulnerable, destitute members cannot finally fend off the God-willed trouble that is here announced. The trouble is sure to come when the city forgets its destiny in fidelity that is God given. So the self-serving that besets Jerusalem becomes a theological crisis of very large proportion, so large that it reaches to the very heart of God. The trouble to come is not in the form of a supernatural pouncing that will come directly from God. The trouble rather is a stunning sociopolitical process whereby the city—now so self-confident and full of itself—has its "first judges restored." That phrase uttered almost in passing is an ominous one in ancient Israel. It refers back to the book of Judges, and that is not good. It is a comment on the breakdown of the urban infrastructure, and a return to the simple, sorry days of turbulence.

The book of Judges is a story of sporadic public leadership exercised by opportunists and thugs, a brand of localism that sounds like street gangs, localism in tension with other localisms, a high level of brutality that culminates in a terrible barbarism against a woman. Life is cheap, and power is careless, and death is always readily at hand. That is how it was with the "former judges," and that is what will come again in the city. The disregard of justice will bring from God a terrible season of threat, danger, and jeopardy.

Of course, this is just poetry from Isaiah. The poet, however, makes a stunning connection: forget the infrastructure of fidelity and what you get is a dog-eat-dog localism in which public dimensions of society evaporate, and each looks only to his or her own narrow interest. That part of the poem could have been uttered yesterday, for it does indeed characterize what is happening in the city. We in our cities regress and return to a kind of local barbarism, because the infrastructure of fidelity is too expensive and calls us to give up our whoring after quick, private solutions.

Then the poet takes a big, deep breath, the kind we are now taking at the end of our binge of self-indulgence. As the threat comes through the poet with a terrible, massive "therefore," so now the newness comes with a breathtaking "afterward." It is a staggering term in the Bible. "Afterward" means there is more that is sure to come that you cannot yet see. What is coming is authorized by God, that is how sure it is. You cannot rush it, and you cannot program it, but must wait and receive as God gives.

The poet dares to imagine and to assert that the appearance of barbarism in the city is not the last turn of affairs. The *afterward* is out of our hands. And that is why I put the title of this sermon as I did. I suspect that George and Bill still belong to the season of regression, for they are prepared to do little to heal the city. I fear they mostly still belong to the season of uncaring exploitation. Of course we must notice and care whether it is Bill or George. It does matter what kind of government we have.

But it matters penultimately. We people who value this poem must think more largely than this slight difference between Bill and George. For the turn of health in the city awaits a different kind of resolve that will never be packaged as a technical fix in a party platform or a governmental policy, urgent as those are. What is required is a new gift of God's grace that is promised, and a fresh embrace of covenantal fidelity that is large and powerful, and sweeps through policy, budget, and institutions.

Afterward—it is promised, it is sure, it is spoken over Jerusalem, and it is uttered over all our treasured Jerusalems.

> Afterward . . . you will be called the city of righteousness,
>   you shall be redeemed by justice
>   and those who live in her who repent, by righteousness.
>   (vv. 26-27)

The poet picks up the terms of the initial covenant of the city. The coming new turn of health in the city is wrought, not by George or by Bill, but by repentance of a public, socio-economic political kind:

- repentence that reengages the *destiny of righteousness*, which entails the valuing of every human life in a way that refuses rapacious exploitation;
- repentance that reembraces the *vocation of justice*, which guarantees the wholeness of life, dignity, and health of all, including widows and orphans, including all the vulnerable and destitute who still hold membership which will not be nullified by disregard or the whoring of self-interest.

Isaiah imagines that the city is to be seen in the large sweep of a dramatic process. The story of the city, the crisis of urbanization, is not told in a few isolated events here and there. The city has an ecology that is definitional, insistent, and resilient. That ecology is to move out of fidelity into self-interest (and we have done that), and a move away from self-interest back into fidelity, and that move is yet in our future . . . afterward.

I imagine that in the story of our United States cities we are yet in the terrible season of "therefore," when God in rage and dismay relinquishes the city to street brutality, greed, fear, and disregard. The "therefore" is powerful and we can see it all around us. And maybe that is all there is. Everyone can see the "therefore" of our cities when the infrastructure of fidelity is ignored.

But we text-people—who treasure the poetry of Isaiah, the promises of Israel and the risks of Jesus—we believe the "therefore" is not the last word, not the end of the poem, not the ultimacy of the city. We believe, even here, in the "afterward". . . new heaven, new earth, new Jerusalem, justice, righteousness, and fidelity.

No more violence,
no more infant mortality,
no more rapacious invasion of the strong against the weak,
no more birthing in pain and labor in vain,
    but all things new.

That is how our mothers and fathers in faith kept on:

They desire a better country, that is, a transcendent one.
Therefore God is not ashamed to be called their God;
    indeed, God has prepared a city for them.
                     (Heb. 11:16)

So we meet on this touchpoint of gospel and city. No doubt we must get the economy moving. No doubt we need better police protection. No doubt the jeopardized black male needs better support. In, with, and under all these unutterable needs, however, is the clue of this poem: The reembrace of fidelity, of membership and entitlement, of all valuing each. That reembrace of fidelity can and will permeate any concrete decision. The promised "afterward" of the vision is no escape. It is rather a resolve, a resolve even in the face of George or Bill. We who trust this poem will not let the city's future of justice and righteousness be reduced to bribes and exploitation. Our insistence is that the city has been misunderstood because the Holy actor at its core has been unnoticed. Where God's "therefore" is unnoticed, God's "afterward" will not be received. But that future is indeed sure . . . and it is coming.

CHAPTER 8

Power to Remember,
Freedom to Forget

Isaiah 51:1-3; 43:15-21, 55:12-13

*Listen to me, you that pursue righteousness,
    you that seek the LORD.
Look to the rock from which you were hewn,
    and to the quarry from which you were dug.
Look to Abraham your father
    and to Sarah who bore you;
for he was but one when I called him,
    but I blessed him and made him many.
For the LORD will comfort Zion;
    he will comfort all her waste places,
and will make her wilderness like Eden,
    her desert like the garden of the LORD;
joy and gladness will be found in her,
    thanksgiving and the voice of song.*

*I am the LORD, your Holy One,
    the Creator of Israel, your King.
Thus says the LORD,
    who makes a way in the sea,
    a path in the mighty waters,
who brings out chariot and horse,
    army and warrior;
they lie down, they cannot rise,*

they are extinguished, quenched like a wick:
Do not remember the former things,
or consider the things of old.
I am about to do a new thing;
now it springs forth, do you not perceive it?
I will make a way in the wilderness
and rivers in the desert.
The wild animals will honor me,
the jackals and the ostriches;
for I give water in the wilderness,
rivers in the desert,
to give drink to my chosen people,
the people whom I formed for myself
so that they might declare my praise.

For you shall go out in joy,
and be led back in peace;
the mountains and the hills before you
shall burst into song,
and all the trees of the field shall clap their hands.
Instead of the thorn shall come up the cypress;
instead of the brier shall come up the myrtle;
and it shall be to the LORD for a memorial,
for an everlasting sign that shall not be cut off.

Texts: Isaiah 51:1-3
Isaiah 43:15-21
Isaiah 55:12-13
Philippians 3:7-16

No one could have foreseen 250 years ago all that would have happened in and through and to this church. No one could have anticipated the wonder of its ministry, the hurts folks have inflicted upon each other, the daring of mission

This sermon was preached in Barrington Congregational Church, Barrington, Rhode Island, on the occasion of the 250th anniversary of the congregation. This congregation not only has a wondrous past to celebrate but also a quite troubled recent history.

enacted, and the fearful, brutalizing world that is now all around us. After so many years (as in ancient Israel) the church in the United States has come to timidity, and society has come to uncaring anxiety. On this high occasion, I reflect on words from Isaiah that sound as though they were written for just such an anniversary as this one.

The poetry of Isaiah knows that in high times and in low times, the community of faith must be engaged in vigorous, active remembering. The poet writes:

> Listen to me, you that pursue righteousness,
>   You that seek the Lord.
> Look to the rock from which you were hewn,
>   and to the quarry from which you were dug.
> Look to Abraham your father and to Sarah who bore you;
>   for he was but one when I called him,
>   but I blessed him and made him many.
>
> (Isa. 51:1-2)

You who seek the Lord, remember your father Abraham and your mother Sarah. This is a highly selective remembering. In any family reunion or any anniversary, some of the ancestors are best forgotten.

The focus is not on a busy, busy chronicle that records everything that happened. Rather this community at risk is invited to focus on the pure models of faithfulness that stand at the head of the parade.

So forget a lot of fathers and remember Abraham and all those fathers of faith in this community who got the thing started against enormous odds. It was Abraham who moved off into the unknown at the call of God, who left what was safe and comfortable for a land whose name he did not even know. It was father Abraham who had the courage to argue with God, who made powerful, daring intercession for the sake of the city of Sodom which had gone wrong. It was father Abraham who was willing to risk his only son and his own future for the sake of full obedience to God. Remember him and all like him in the past of his church.

Remember Sarah your mother in faith. It was Sarah in her old age who laughed in scorn at God's promise. But she was convicted by the power of God and transformed. She birthed a son in her old age, created a future, and served God's impossibility in the world. This is a model for resurrection faith, because she came to believe and trust that God could create newness out of defeat, barrenness, and even death.

This is the day and the time and the year when the people of God in this place remember fathers in faith who risked and dared and obeyed, who cared for the city gone awry. This is the day for remembering mothers in faith who laughed in and for God's power for new life. The names of mothers and fathers have sometimes been forgotten. For that reason, stories must be told and jokes enjoyed from the past, and pictures shown, while all this old, powerful stuff surges into the present and evokes wonder at what the mothers and fathers in this place did, and gratitude for their courage and freedom, and awe at the miracle of what God has done through them.

Remembering of this sort can correct two misperceptions:

1. We live in a society that remembers almost nothing, and our children are mostly committed to a careless amnesia. Indeed, one little girl said she knew about the history of the early church: "It all began in 1935, when my pastor was born." But if we imagine that we can scuttle all the old shaping and treat the church as thinly present-tense, then we can imagine that the church is putty in our hands. The church, however, has long, time-tested shapes for mission and faith, shapes that summon and continue to shape our faith and to require of us.

2. The other reason for remembering is that if we forget, then we imagine that the church was only a lucky break, a stumbling accident. In fact, every congregation has at its origin and at its great missional moments some daring people with intensity and passion who have cared and insisted and sacrificed with vision. This great church stands on the shoulders of mothers and fathers who have

been obedient to the gospel in ways that matter. So remember these great saints in this church, but also remember around the edges of this church, all sorts of old Congregationalists who cared, and old Evangelicals and old Reformed folk, all of whom belong to the family of the United Church of Christ, this family of risk and obedience, all of whom are in the woodwork around us today. Remember, give thanks, be amazed, and sign on with their passions.

This same poet to this same people in exile uttered a second urging that moves against the first one:

> Do not remember the former things,
>   or consider the things of old.
> I am about to do a new thing;
>   now it springs forth, do you not perceive it?
> I make a way in the wilderness
>   and rivers in the desert.
> The wild animals will honor me,
>   the jackals and ostriches,
> for I give water in the wilderness,
>   rivers in the desert,
> to give drink to my chosen people.
>
> (Isa. 43:18-20)

There is a danger that on an anniversary occasion we become excessively nostalgic and romantic for the good old days, when usually, by the good old days, we mean only about thirty-two years ago. I was for some time a pastor in a congregation of the United Church of Christ in New York City that was nearly defunct. Every year at strawberry time, the church had a strawberry festival. In prior years they used to fill the church basement with excitement, delight, and many people. Now only about twenty-four people came; all the others were gone. But in an act of nostalgia, they continued the pretense and set up tables for two hundred people, with many uneaten strawberries.

Isaiah writes about this people so excessively in love with those wonderful past times that they have completely misunderstood the present tense. These ancient Israelites, six hundred years later, loved to talk about the exodus and God's powerful, old intervention for freedom. And so it goes on as a community of memory, about the wonderful long ago when somebody did something special.

But God says to them, "Do not remember former things." That is, forget! Forget the past and the memory—why? Because "I am doing a new thing," a new liberation, a new history, a new home-coming.

Anniversaries are times to drink deeply of the past and then, before the celebration is over, to turn your mind and your heart and your attention away from the past into the present, which belongs to God, and into the future where God is calling us to a deep and different newness.

The new thing for ancient Jews was the liberation from Babylon, which was to eclipse for them even the Egyptian exodus, so don't talk about the Exodus any more, talk about Babylon. The new thing for early Christians was the new healing, liberating work of Jesus, so don't talk any more about the old story, talk about what Jesus did. And now, for us? For this great church at the turn into God's future?

Let me hazard a word about the new thing of God which is to cause us to forget the old wonders. We have come off a certain ordering of social reality that has been long established and which seemed right, a relation of privilege and poverty, of power and pain, and we learned how to manage that arrangement. It does seem as though the lid has blown off that arrangement: the old privileges of wealth and power lack credibility, the old authority of whites and males is trembling, the old advantage of European rootage and all the rest is in deep jeopardy. And it makes us very frightened.

God is indeed doing a new thing among us. God is fashioning a new pattern of social relations in which privilege will have to attend to poverty, in which power will have to submit to pain, in which advantage will have to be recruited for compassion, in which old priorities will have to be repositioned in order to let in people long kept out. God is doing a new thing. Let me tell you three things about this new thing:

1. The loss of the old scares all of us, liberal and conservative, because we feel threatened and displaced. And that loss causes us to do anxious, mean, and selfish things to each other, things that live at the edge of brutality. It will be useful in our turn to the future on this anniversary day to notice the high level of stress that the loss of the old produces and to honor each other in our fear and our anxiety.

2. Nobody knows the shape of the newness. That is what produces the uncertainty and anxiety. I believe that in all the great public, missional issues, we will live for a while between the times, until God's spirit leads us into a freshly formed life together. That anticipation of God's newness requires alert watching for glimpses of God's work and God's will.

3. The newness of God seldom comes without obedient human investment. That is where the church comes in. This church is not permitted by God to sit around in its building and its reputation, but is summoned by God to

- be at work for God's current newness
- think with the riskiness of father Abraham and to receive with the delight of mother Sarah
- be the womb for birthing a new wonder in the world, rivers in the desert, a genuine human home in an arena of stark fear. This of course will require the church to think quite freshly toward the future, and think very large about its mission in the city and in the world. It is for this that you have been called.

Thus an anniversary is a time to get one's mind off old hurts and old quarrels, and get refocused on the call of God. The poet chides Israel and says, "I am doing a new thing. Do you not perceive it?" Can't you notice it? Won't you look again?

Anniversaries take the form of a parade, an exuberant procession on its way somewhere. Anniversaries are not for sitting in one's place, but for coming and going, departing and arriving. So the poet concludes:

> For you shall go out in joy,
>> and be led back in peace . . .
> Instead of the thorn shall come up the cypress;
>> instead of the brier shall come up the myrtle;
> and it shall be to the Lord for a memorial,
>> for an everlasting sign that shall not be cut off.
>> (Isa. 55:12-13)

Go out in joy and in peace, not in anxiety nor in discomfort. Go out, taking your life transformed from brier to cypress, from prickly brier to a blooming flower tree.

So dear people of Barrington Congregational, go out. Go out from old, tired stuff, go out from fears that divide you, go out from old quarrels unresolved. Go out from old sins unforgiven. Go out from old decisions that have scarred and wounded. Go out from old memories that have become graven images. Go out into God's new, demanding mission.

- Go the way of father Abraham, to a new way and place of life.
- Go out laughing like mother Sarah, surprised by new life.
- Go out to neighbors waiting for a caring act of generosity.

As you go, singing, celebrating, and grateful, imagine concretely and know that

- the mission of this church is not finished,
- the work of this church is not a holding action,
- the future of this church is not business as usual.

What if your departing to the future is done around some great dramatic missional gesture, some stunning act of generosity, some large enterprise undertaken, some major dollars given away to neighbors, so that on the five hundredth anniversary, this daring act will be the old, old story that becomes the new, new song.

There is a danger in forgetting what you must remember,
There is a danger in remembering what you must forget,
There is a danger in staying when you must depart in faith.

Anniversaries are wonderful events for regrouping, with gifts of courage and energy and freedom freshly given and not squeezed into old patterns.

Now I am finished, except for the good word from Paul that sounds like an anniversary text:

> Not that I have already obtained or have already reached the goal; but I press on to make it my own, because Christ Jesus has made me his own. Beloved, I do not consider that I have made it my own; but this one thing I do: forgetting what lies behind and striving forward to what lies ahead, I press on toward the goal for the prize of the call of God in Christ Jesus. Let those of us then who are mature be of the same mind.
>
> (Phil. 3:12-15)

On this day, do passionate remembering, liberated forgetting, and, finally, joyous departing.

9

Outrageous God,
Season of Decrease

Isaiah 65:17-25

For I am about to create new heavens
and a new earth;
the former things shall not be remembered
or come to mind.
But be glad and rejoice forever
in what I am creating;
for I am about to create Jerusalem as a joy,
and its people as a delight.
I will rejoice in Jerusalem,
and delight in my people;
no more shall the sound of weeping be heard in it,
or the cry of distress.
No more shall there be in it
an infant that lives but a few days,
or an old person who does not live out a lifetime;
for one who dies at a hundred years will be considered
a youth,
and one who falls short of a hundred will be considered
accursed.
They shall build houses and inhabit them;
they shall plant vineyards and eat their fruit.
They shall not build and another inhabit;
they shall not plant and another eat;

for like the days of a tree shall the days of my people be,
and my chosen shall long enjoy the work of their hands.
They shall not labor in vain,
or bear children for calamity;
for they shall be offspring blessed by the LORD—
and their descendants as well.
Before they call I will answer,
while they are yet speaking I will hear.
The wolf and the lamb shall feed together,
the lion shall eat straw like the ox;
but the serpent—its food shall be dust!
They shall not hurt or destroy
on all my holy mountain,
says the LORD.

Texts: Isaiah 65:17-25
1 Thessalonians 5:16-28
John 3:23-30

There is something deeply outrageous about Advent, which is made clear in this poem of Isaiah 65. It is so outrageous that none of us really believes it. Nonetheless, we are the baptized people who have promised to share such a text, such a vision.

So I invite you to entertain for a moment this poem, and let it seep into your bones and into your heart and into your vision. God speaks: "New heaven, new earth, new Jerusalem." It will be a world of rejoicing when the newness comes. And do you know why?

Heaven and earth will rejoice because, in that new world wrought by God, there will be no more the sound of weeping, no

This sermon was preached at the Cathedral of St. Philip in Atlanta on the third Sunday in Advent.

more homeless folks to moan, no more broken folk to whimper, no more terrorized folk to cry out.

Heaven and earth will rejoice, because in that new world wrought by God there will be no more infant mortality, no more infants who live but a few days, and no more old people who will die too young or live too feebly or continue as a shell while the life is gone.

Heaven and earth will rejoice, because in that new world wrought by God there will be no more usurpation of peoples' homes. Those who build will stay around to inhabit, those who plant will survive to harvest and enjoy their produce. No more people being taxed out of their homes, no more losing their vulnerable homes to the right of eminent domain, no more rapacious seizure by war, no more the big ones eating the little ones. When the newness comes, every person will live safely under a vine and fig tree, safe, unafraid, at peace, no more destructive threat nor competitive anxiety.

Heaven and earth will rejoice, because in that new world. wrought by God, there will be no more labor in vain, no more birthing into anguish, no more nurturing children in anxiety and dread and fear, because God will bless and make the force of life everywhere palpably available. Persons and families will live in well-being, without jeopardy or grief.

Heaven and earth will rejoice, because in that new world wrought by God, God will be attentive. God will be like a mother who hears and answers in the night, knowing before we call who is needed and what is needed. And we shall never be left alone again.

I told you it was outrageous. It is outrageous because the new world of God is beyond our capacity and even beyond our imagination. It does not seem possible. In our fatigue, our self-sufficiency, and our cynicism, we deeply believe that such promises could not happen here. Such newness is only poetic fantasy, and there are the persistent realities of injustice and grief and terror, and it will never end, not in any future we can conjure.

In Advent, however, we receive the power of God that lies beyond us. We receive it willingly, because it is the evangelical antidote to our fatigue and cynicism. We grasp hold eagerly, because it is the gospel resolution to our spent self-sufficiency, when we are at the edge of our coping. We seize the vision in craving, because it is the good news that will overmatch our cynicism that imagines there is no new thing that can enter our world.

This poet does the proper work of poetry, inviting us to cut free beyond ourselves and to entertain the notion that other purposes for goodness and other power for healing and other promise for *shalom* are indeed loosed in the world. Advent is a pondering of this outrageousness that will outflank our weary Christmas.

Into this world of lyrical poetry, says our Gospel, pushes the unkempt, unwelcome figure of John the Baptizer. You remember him. He is dressed in hair shirt. He eats wild honey and such other gifts that he can forage in the rough. He comes in anger and demand, and threat and insistence. He speaks really only one word: *Repent!* Recognize the danger you are in and change.

In the Gospel narrative, John embodies the best and the last of the old tradition of Torah demand. He has this deep sense of urgency about the world, but it is not an urgency of newness. It is an urgency of threat and danger and jeopardy, one that we ourselves sense now about our world. He comes first in the story. He comes before Jesus. He is the key player in the Advent narrative.

When Jesus appears on the scene, John the Baptizer immediately acknowledges the greatness of Jesus, greater than all that is past— greater than John, greater than all ancient memories and hopes. When Jesus comes into the narrative, John quickly, abruptly, without reservation says of Jesus, "He must increase, I must decrease."

So here is what we have. We have heard this poem that we take to be outrageous, so overwhelming is it in its claim. There is not much to do about that large vision, except to wait for it and to watch for it. But what to do while we watch and wait? Move from the large vision to the small discipline of John. If John embodies all that is old and Jesus embodies all that is new, take as your Advent work toward Christmas that enterprise: decrease/increase. Decrease what is old and habitual and destructive in your life, so that the new life-giving power of Jesus may grow large with you.

- Decrease what is greedy, what is frantic consumerism, for the increase of simple, life-giving sharing.
- Decrease what is fearful and defensive, for the increase of life-giving compassion and generosity.
- Decrease what is fraudulent and pretense, for the increase of life-giving truth-telling in your life, truth-telling about you and your neighbor, about the sickness of our society and our enmeshment in that sickness.
- Decrease what is hateful and alienating, for the increase of healing and forgiveness, which finally are the only source of life.

Advent basks in the great promises. In the meantime, however, there are daily disciplines, day-to-day exercises of Advent, work that requires time and intentionality, that has nothing to do with the busyness that the world imposes upon us. God will do much to bring the promises to fruition. But God will not do our work of redeciding our life. There is for us, only us, the staggering possibility of choosing real life and turning away from the killing in which we are much practiced.

Advent is not for sitting around, but it is for pondering and noticing, embracing, renouncing, and receiving. We watch while we notice the increase of gospel living, of sharing, of growing in compassion, of generosity, of hope, of truth-telling, in healing and in forgiveness. Such a newness!

As the gifts of the gospel embodied in Jesus may increase for us, something peculiar and cosmic happens in our midst. We begin to hear the rustle of new heaven and new earth, new Jerusalem and new Atlanta, and it does not now sound so outrageous in its coming. We move toward the vision and ponder the poem and notice the news around us.

Advent is not a time of casual waiting. It is a demanding piece of work. It requires that we attend to both the outrageousness of God and the daily work of decreasing. The outcome of such Advent goes like this. Listen:

> They shall not hurt or destroy
> in all my holy mountain, says the Lord. (v. 25)

That will be some newness! Some Christmas! Some gospel!

10

God's Relentless "If"

Jeremiah 5:20-29

Declare this in the house of Jacob,
proclaim it in Judah:
Hear this, O foolish and senseless people,
who have eyes, but do not see,
who have ears, but do not hear.
Do you not fear me? says the LORD;
Do you not tremble before me?
I placed the sand as a boundary for the sea,
a perpetual barrier that it cannot pass;
though the waves toss, they cannot prevail,
though they roar, they cannot pass over it.
But this people has a stubborn and rebellious heart;
they have turned aside and gone away.
They do not say in their hearts,
"Let us fear the LORD *our God,*
who gives the rain in its season,
the autumn rain and the spring rain,
and keeps for us
the weeks appointed for the harvest."
Your iniquities have turned these away,
and your sins have deprived you of good.
For scoundrels are found among my people;
they take over the goods of others.

> Like fowlers they set a trap;
>> they catch human beings.
> Like a cage full of birds,
>> their houses are full of treachery;
> therefore they have become great and rich,
>> they have grown fat and sleek.
> They know no limits in deeds of wickedness;
>> they do not judge with justice
> the cause of the orphan, to make it prosper,
>> and they do not defend the rights of the needy.
> Shall I not punish them for these things?
>> says the LORD,
> and shall I not bring retribution
> on a nation such as this?

Text: Jeremiah 5:20-29

Already with Moses, God has said that the status of Israel depends upon an enormous "If":

> Therefore, if you obey my voice and keep my covenant, you shall be my treasured possession out of all the peoples.
>
> (Exod. 19:5)

And God said *sotto voce*, "If you don't, you won't." Even with the great King Solomon, the relentless "if" made its heavy sound in the context of royal self-assurance. David, the father of the great King, taught his son:

> If your heirs take heed to their way, to walk before me in faithfulness with all their heart and with all their life, there shall not fail you a successor on the throne of Israel (1 Kings 2:4). . . . [But if they don't, they won't].

This sermon was preached at Lexington Theological Seminary, Lexington, Kentucky as part of the Leslie R. Smith Lectures that the author gave on Jeremiah.

And what father David had said to son Solomon was intensified in God's own speech to the king with a double "if":

> As for you, if you will walk before me, as David your father walked, with integrity of heart and uprightness, doing according to all that I have commanded you . . . then I will establish your royal throne forever. . . . There shall not fail you a successor on the throne of Israel.
>
> (1 Kings 9:4-5)

And this time, the negative "if" is not implied or said under breath, but made quite explicit:

> If you turn aside from following me, you or your children, and do not keep my commandments and my statutes that I have set before you . . . then I will cut Israel off from the land that I gave them. . . .
>
> (1 Kings 9:6-7)

That "if" of conditional moral insistence looms large and definitional over the life and faith of Israel. In the very fabric of this faith is the awareness that it costs to live with God. It costs to live in God's world.

And now that "if" looms large and threatening for us, even in this "therapeutic culture" of ours. We do not want it to be so, but we soon and late rush our heads against the wall of God's conditionality, and it does not yield. I submit that for people of faith, and for people who want to survive humanely, what we do with that hard, uncompromising "if" is an issue that needs powerful, attentive pastoral processing.

I take your time with the book of Jeremiah, because I dare imagine that this text of Jeremiah is pertinent and poignant for us. The world of Jeremiah (so disturbingly reflected in the book of Jeremiah) was coming unglued, by internal neglect and abdication, by moral cynicism among the powerful, and by external threat. Most astonishing is that while this was going on, nobody noticed:

> . . . who have eyes, but do not see,
>   who have ears, but do not hear.
>   (Jer. 5:21)

What kept them from seeing? It was the time when the Jerusalem establishment in all its complacency was coming to an end. They were in the season of "the last king," but they thought a "last king" was simply not possible. They did not notice, because what was happening was "impossible" and did not admit of acknowledgment. What kept them from hearing? They watched the Assyrians vanish quickly; they watched the Babylonians arise from nowhere; they witnessed the rise and fall of superpowers in one generation. They were, however, numbed and falsely assured by their faith and their worldview, and so they heard nothing. They never noticed, because their casual, uncritical faith had become for them a narcotic. It encouraged and legitimated their self-deception and denial and numbness.

They never noticed, never saw, and never heard. In that context, this book of Jeremiah stands like an oddity, a voice that noticed. This Jeremiah is not a lone individual against the system. That is too easy and too romantic. It is rather the voice of *a countertradition*, a line of teaching and perception not so fully seduced by the unconditional promises floating around in Jerusalem. Jeremiah is informed by a tradition of faith located outside the city and its ideology. It has another point of reference all the way back to the memory and authority of Moses. It is a hard, demanding theological tradition, mostly unwelcome, but it is nonetheless the core tradition that gives Israel its vocation and its staying power. In that countertradition of Moses, at the center of his utterance, was this hard "if," uttered by the God who refused to be domesticated. It is an "if" reflecting God's freedom and God's sovereignty, God's moral demand—a God refusing to be mocked or to give in to the easier faith of complacency and accommodation. Jeremiah hears in his head and in his city the pounding of the Mosaic "if."

It is this "if" given by Moses that put the city of Jerusalem under threat. It was not the failure of kings nor the invading armies, but the uncompromising requirement of Yahweh that recast the situation of Jerusalem. It is, moreover, that same "if" that gives identity and force to the man Jeremiah and the text of Jeremiah. It is that terrible "if" that causes Jeremiah to see and hear and notice and care, that haunts him in the night and that goads him all the day long to say what must be said. It is that terrible "if" that cannot be tolerated by his contemporaries.

This inescapable "if" puts the troubled voice of Jeremiah in such a crunch. It would be better not to know, not to see, not to hear. But having known, the poet cannot un-know. Better not to see; but having seen, the prophet cannot un-see. Better not to hear; but having heard, Jeremiah cannot un-hear. This voice in this terrible text speaks not because it is angry or liberal or radical or hired or bribed, but because this awesome knowing and seeing and hearing require utterance. It is an unwelcome utterance, almost certain to fail. Its only purpose is to sound the unbearable "if" that insists upon moral reality that cannot be evaded, cannot be outflanked by policy, cannot be outvoted by popular opinion. This moral danger has such staying power because it is rooted in God's own life and God's own purpose. And it must be spoken, out loud, in this city numbed by its narcoticizing habits.

The text invites us into an odd situation. There is an uncaring, unnoticing public on its uncaring way to ruin. And there is this voice-in-text that must witness underneath the numbness, seeking to talk sense to those most uninterested in any serious sense-making. How to speak in that context, sure to be rejected? How odd that the strategy of Jeremiah is not didactic, not heavy-handed morality, not even policy debate about war-readiness. Instead, what we get in this most implausible situation is poetry, only poetry. The man and the book have a vocation of poetry that is daring on two counts.

- This practice of poetry is, in its form and shape, odd, jarring, surging with subversive images, refusing to accept the conventions of speech and the categories of perception that are usual and expected. It is the work of such poetry to require people to see what they are determined to avoid. Jeremiah is consummately skillful in requiring notice, and in the process, dismantling the safe world of unreality in which official Jerusalem loved to traffic.

- This practice of poetry is odd, because the subject of the poetry is this God of the "if." In the poetry, this God dares to speak first-person. There is no debate here about the "inspiration and revelation and authority" of the text, but simply a direct, intentional, abrupt "declare this/hear this" (v. 20). The cadences of Jeremiah turn out to be the utterance of the great sovereign one who presides over the "if," and by this utterance plunges the holy city into the midst of its ungluing. Do you wonder in our secularism how God can come again to be effectively present in the midst of our numbed cities? The word is, in the same way (by the hutzpah of poets who offer no intellectual justification, but who utter what must be uttered), on the very lips of God. The poet imagines, or claims, or pretends to have drawn close to the voice and mouth and heart of God, and to give God speech. It is a sound so unwelcome in Jerusalem, unwelcome because it is so incongruous with what we had hoped and seized for ourselves. But it is sounded!

God speaks here in such an odd voice, a word so unsettling. When the poet voices the sounds of God, this is what gets said:

> hear this . . . stupid folk, you who are drugged in indifference;
> hear this . . . you who do not know you are the ones addressed;
> hear this . . . "Do you not fear me?"
>
> (vv. 21-22a)

We are not talking here of reverence or awe. We are talking about raw terror. "Are you not properly scared of me, as you ought to be? Do I not make you tremble, tremble, tremble? Am I not fierce or real enough for you to recognize your true situation of jeopardy before me?"

Notice what has happened in this city now under poetic assault. In its profound amnesia, having long since forgotten the counter-tradition of Moses, it had not seemed to beleaguered Jerusalem that Yahweh was even a player in its destiny. Yahweh gets back into the game only because of the poet who now "re-speaks" the God of Sinai. All it takes for God to reenter the public arena as sovereign threat is a memory and a tongue, a text and a measure of courage; and the future of Jerusalem is set in drastically, abruptly different categories.

Why fear me? Because I am the one who has tamed chaos (v. 22b). I am the one so strong, so bold, so large, so authoritative, so resolved; I fend off chaos, I order the floods, I stop the power of death, I draw a line against the deathly waters and say, "Come no further." I did it in creation, I did it in Easter, and I do it all the time. I am the one who acts in magisterial ways to give you a safe place for life, and your life depends upon my capacity to resist the powers of chaos. I act for you in all my sovereign power, and you do not notice enough to fear me, to tremble before me, to notice the majestic splendor of my way that is well beyond your manipulation.

This pitiful, numbed crowd in Jerusalem, so self-convinced, self-preoccupied, self-sufficient, is not able to make a connection with vitality and fruitfulness and abundance and rain (v. 24). That crowd could not see that its own local, immediate setting in Jerusalem is in the midst of the creation that God has ordered and made possible and guaranteed. That crowd could not admit that disregarding God would cause drought, because God gives rain. They could not remember that the chance for life in creation depends upon keeping Torah, which is the concrete way of obeying creator and honoring creation. In their passion for their own technical control, the crowd in Jerusalem could not compute that at the core of their existence lay a guaranteeing mystery—a mystery that costs. They could not see the linkage, the irrefutable link between the richness of creation and the "if" of Torah. The connections were too primitive and too prerational for their flat, simplistic calculations. And so the connections must be made in another way, this time in the flimsiness of a poem. So the poem runs from chaos to drought, in the center of which looms this God who will be taken seriously.

But the problem that now jeopardizes the city is not a large disregard of creation. That is too cosmic for this poet or the God he speaks. The problem for biblical faith is always more concrete. When the moral shape of reality is disregarded, the crisis does not show up in some generalized way. It shows up, characteristically, as *neighbor crisis*. The poet becomes quite specific in his expose of the "if-less" city:

> Like fowlers they set a trap;
>   they catch human beings.
> Like a cage full of birds. . . .
>   (vv. 26b-27a)

They use and abuse and oppress and exploit because, without an "if," everything is possible—greed, brutality, despair, all of it, with the neighbor as target. In our stupidity, these folk do not look like neighbors that are protected by God's "if." They look only like an inconvenience, or even a threat.

And, you guessed it: This whole abusive insensitivity comes down, as it always does, to economics. It does not come down to sexuality or to purity or to private morality, but to dollar power and dollar manipulation:

> Therefore they have become great and rich,
>   they have grown fat and sleek,
> They know no limits in deeds of wickedness;
>   they do not judge with justice
>   the cause of the orphan, to make it prosper,
>   and they do not defend the rights of the needy.
>   (vv. 27b-28)

They are fat, rich, and sleek, so they do not care about the needy,

> not about health care,
> not about housing,
> not about education,
> not about anything.

When God is cheapened, neighbors become inexpensive. When God and neighbor disappear,

> the city will fail,
> the rain will stop,
> the world will fall apart,
> the neighbor will die.

"If-lessness" will not finally work; it is a path of self-destructiveness. The poet makes a very quick, very large travel from the God who tames chaos (v. 22) to the crisis of drought (v. 24) to economic abuse of neighbor (vv. 26-28). In such a quick review, the poet places on God's lips the assertion of a connection between specific neighbor care and the vast problem of chaos and order. And between the specific neighbor and the large order of the cosmos is the problem of drought and the undoing of a "sustainable creation." It is all there, all held together, in five quick verses, all an invitation for the numbed city to awaken, for those who refuse to see and to fear and to tremble. The awakening is to the raw fact that all the self-preoccupation has not driven God's relentless "if" off the map. That "if" stays there at center, looming, waiting for its just due.

Finally, the poet has God draw upon the most powerful rhetoric with which to conclude the poem. We expect a great, harsh verdict, some massive, uncompromising "therefore." But what we get, instead, is a question on the tongue of God:

> Shall I not punish them for these things? (v. 29)

Some question from the throat of the Holy One! We cannot tell from the text the tone of the question. I think of three options in inflecting the question:

1. It may be a fierce, defiant, scornful voicing, turned to an indicative: Of course I must punish, and I will! How could you imagine otherwise?
2. It might be a pleading, plaintiff, wounded option, wishing that punishment could be avoided. This voicing would be an asking, "Is there not another way around? Must I do now what seems to follow, because I wish I did not have to do it?"
3. It may be a genuine, serious question. Is that what follows? Is it time now to implement the sanctions of this uncompromising "if"?

The poet lets us play with this last line of the poem. I suspect that God plays with it as well, because it is too awesome. There is too much at risk. Is this the end of it all? Does the covenant end in severity, a severity already set in motion by the uncompromising utterance of Moses at Sinai? Is that all there is? We wonder, as God must.

The listeners to Jeremiah in Jerusalem came very close to finding out the answer to God's haunting question in the events of 587 B.C.E. And so may we receive an answer to the same question in our unglued setting. I would not extrapolate and "apply" the text, because I think Jeremiah does not want to be "applied." Jeremiah reached back all the way to Moses for this devastating but realistic "if." We ponder in our own context: Does Jeremiah also reach forward all the way to us? Is this terrible "if" swirling around our emptied politics and our failed social fabric? Is our scene so emptied and failed that it is now incapable of hosting moral shape and moral cost and moral possibility? Is it no longer possible to see, like a hologram, that the whole scope of creation and chaos is present in the most concrete neighbor transaction? This is not an intramural theological question asked for the entertainment of seminarians and the intellectual verve of their teachers. This is now a large, critical issue that concerns all who inhabit the threatened city. The question is, What is the world like? The question, "Shall I not punish them?" might well haunt us, because we do not know the tone of its asking.

If this question is to haunt us—not scare us, not scold us, not judge us, but haunt us—it will happen only as the community of this text can still remember what our society chooses no longer to notice. The question bites deep for us personally, because we know about unglued worlds. We all know about them in ways that haunt deeply. But the larger issue for us is our vocation as the church to the world. There is here, perhaps, a mandate for haunting poetry that lets us see and hear and notice in our stupidity.

We are, I imagine, like old Jerusalem. The very poetry we dread and want to silence is the poetry we must hear—and utter. We must utter it, because the God of Moses has no other access point in the unglued city, except to haunt with trembling by poetic lips. Those lips do indeed cause a deep trembling, for the one who utters and for those who hear.

PART THREE
Texts from the Writings

CHAPTER 11
A Bilingual Life

Job 26:1-3; 27:1-6

Then Job answered:
> *"How you have helped one who has no power!*
> *How you have assisted the arm that has no strength!*
> *How you have counseled one who has no wisdom,*
> > *and given much good advice!*

Job again took up his discourse and said:
> *"As God lives, who has taken away my right,*
> > *and the Almighty, who has made my soul bitter,*
> *as long as my breath is in me*
> > *and the spirit of God is in my nostrils,*
> *my lips will not speak falsehood,*
> > *and my tongue will not utter deceit.*
> *Far be it from me to say that you are right;*
> > *until I die I will not put away my integrity from me.*
> *I hold fast my righteousness, and will not let it go;*
> > *my heart does not reproach me for any of my days."*

Texts: Job 26:1-3; 27:1-6
Mark 10:17-22

ob's problem is that he cannot find an adequate conversation partner. Job finds his friends, models of scrupulousness, boring and unconvincing. Job mocks them for their lack of persuasiveness:

> How you have helped him who has no power!
> How you have saved the one that has no strength!
> How you have counseled him who has no wisdom,
>   and plentifully declared sound knowledge!
>
> (26:2-3a)

Job dismisses the friends with dripping sarcasm and scorn. Their "fortune cookie" theology has not shaken Job's sense of justice, nor his conviction of his own innocence. Their argument seems designed only to undermine his self-confidence, shatter his self-esteem, and make him feel bad. Job, however, is tough. He will not fold. After his rebuke of them, the friends do not speak again. We may forget about them. Small-minded moral scrupulousness is driven from the field. It is no adequate way to live, and it has no place in the poem.

Our hero is not overly scrupulous. He is, however, a man of virtue and integrity, judged by any available standard. He has been so from the first verse of Job; and no evidence has been brought against him. He is as good in chapter 27 as the narrator announced him to be in chapter 1. Job knows his virtue; so he vows an oath of defiance and self-confidence:

> As God lives . . .
>   as long as I have breath,
>   I will not speak falsehood.
>
> (27:2-4)

This sermon was preached during a summer session at Columbia Theological Seminary.

He means falsehood that denied his virtue. He will not falsely present himself. He will not knuckle under. He will not commit perjury against himself. He swears by the very God who has not played fair, the God who has "taken away my right." Job asserts, "I will not pretend guilt where there is none. I will not submit against the known data of my own life." Then he swears a second, sweeping oath concerning his friends:

> Far be it from me to say you are right.
> Till I die, I will not put away my integrity from me.
>   I will hold fast to my righteousness.
> I will not relinquish it.
>
> (27:5-6a)

I will not be talked out of what I know. I will not engage in submission on false grounds, not just to accommodate religious convention. If Job were not so good, he would be arrogant. But he is good. He is morally good. He is theologically good, discerning, and responsible. He knows what serious theology is all about. He understands what healthy humanness costs. He is an embodiment of integrity, of wholeness, completeness. He knows how to "will one thing." That one thing he has willed and lived is a responsible, caring, compassionate, generous life. Not many of us would ever be cast in the role of Job. He is nonetheless a model. His figure is thinkable. We could imagine such a person. The poet affirms that we can at least imagine a model of humanity who has it right with God and with neighbor. We are created for a caring, responsible life of integrity.

Thus Jesus dared to say to his disciples, "Be perfect, as your father is perfect." Jesus uses the same words as Moses. Moses said, "Be blameless before the Lord your God." Jesus said, Be perfect, be blameless, have integrity, will one thing. It is do-able and you should do it.

If that were enough, however, there would be no poem of Job. We would have stopped with the piety and faith of chapter 2. We would have saved ourselves a lot of trouble. Job pushes beyond the command of classic convenantal faith. Job's pain runs past Deuteronomy, because the poet has grasped the point: A life of integrity, of getting it right and living it well, in the end is not enough. It is not enough, because trouble comes. It is not enough, because friends scold and correct. Mainly, however, it is not enough because we are created and ordained for a deeper, more demanding restlessness. It is that other restlessness beyond virtue, so elusive and so urgent, that both satisfies us and places us in crisis. That restlessness beyond virtue is a yearning for a conversation, a communion, a transaction that outruns integrity and is not preoccupied with our goodness. Goodness is not enough, and in the end it is as uninteresting as it is unsatisfying.

The long sweep of the poem of Job is the attempt to find another conversation partner. Job is Adam *redux*. Adam seeks a partner among all the animals, and finally settles on the woman. Job seeks a conversation partner who will address him at the point of his anguish. The friends will not address him in his anguish, but will only rebuke him. Job must, however, find a partner who is not oversimple, boring, unconvincing. He must find a partner worthy of his life, elusive enough to interest, hidden enough to attract, severe enough to detain, awesome enough to counter. He must find one or he is left with only his integrity. His integrity is real and important, but it is not adequate for the living of his life. The trial of Job's existence is that he cannot summon nor produce nor conjure this other voice of restlessness that will keep his life open. He must wait and the waiting makes him only more restless.

Then, after the long wait of thirty-seven chapters, comes the voice unexpected and unexplained, not evoked by Job's insistence, not sponsored by Job's integrity, from an unknown region, without cause or motivation, simply present and sounding overwhelming. Job is addressed by the "thereness" of God who is simply there, there before Job and after Job, but also there for Job. God is there for Job, but refuses to engage Job on Job's terms. Astonishingly and against his reckoning, Job is drawn into another conversation that he has not anticipated and that he could not manage. With the friends, Job knew how the talk would end before it began. He cannot, however, see through this exchange. The language of integrity and virtue and moral responsibility and ethical calculations is now excluded and superseded. This "other restlessness" will not speak in those categories. Instead there is the language of power, awe, mystery, amazement, daring, astonishment, miracle, the inscrutable lyrical language of doxology—on the very lips of God. It is language that is raw, unencumbered, dangerous—on the very lips of God. Job finds himself in a conversation beyond any he had imagined or wanted. Job had known how to do doxology, but he had forgotten liberated praise when he was pressed too close and thought he had to defend himself.

The poem of Job is put together to assert that Job's integrity, crucial as it is, is penultimate. His integrity lives tentatively in front of doxology. Job stands before the one who asks sovereign questions, who calls to account, who blows Job off the map by daring to show how limited and contained is Job's field of vision. The speech of this Other who wants praise and not virtue, yielding and not bargaining, risk and not answers, this other speech recontextualizes Job's integrity. Yes, hang on to your integrity, Job, for it is never questioned. But learn a second language. Learn to speak praise and yielding which let you cherish your virtue less tightly. Job said, "I will hold fast to my integrity until I die." Well, hold on too tight and you will die soon, because such integrity becomes a screen against the awesome reality of God. And when cut off from God, even by virtue, you will die, bored, self-satisfied, utterly unsatisfied with an unresolved restlessness.

The battle to be fought in the church now, in our society generally, is for speech and faith that will sustain us. Job, and even more his friends, are models of ideological certitude.

That kind of moral certitude, however, does not matter ultimately, because we are not saved by our virtue. No one can stand in the face of the whirlwind on a soap-box of virtue. Virtue has many ideological faces in our society—and they all kill. It may be the over-scrupulousness about sexuality and piety and all those treasured old-fashioned virtues. Or it may be the ideological agenda of the right, getting things settled about prayer in the public schools or homosexuality or the Panama Canal. Or it may be the strident programs of the left and being correct about abortion and welfare and divestment. Whichever party we belong to, we hold it all dear and precious and we brood in our virtue, confident that the others are without credibility.

Job learned what we all learn sooner or later. Virtue does not suffice. Integrity does not give life. Being right is no substitute for being amazed. Controlling will not substitute for yielding in awe and wonder and amazement. The shift to Job's other language is practically urgent, as it is theologically imperative. The shift to doxology as a mode of life is theologically imperative because praise breaks our terrible idolatries. We live in a society of preferred virtues, of convinced moralities, of exacting, relentless idolatries. As with Job, these idols of self-congratulations block healing, make us falsely at ease, prevent transformation, and reduce life to a set of slogans and technologies.

The alternative good news of the poem is that we are made for a second conversation that surprises us and that we can never anticipate. After our earnest behavior, we are invited to doxological yielding. The shift in language destabilizes us, puts us at risk, debunks our control, eases our need to dominate, and lets us yield without pouting, submit without resentment, and receive as gift a new restlessness that is communion and praise.

After the yielding lyric, we are like Job. We still must go home and live as virtuously as possible. We have, however, been decisively intruded upon, invaded, overwhelmed, reduced to stunned silence, taken seriously by eternity, and finally, like Job, approved in our virtue (42:7-8).

We and Job are like the rich young ruler (Mark 10:17-22). The commandments still pertain. The commandments are what we must do to inherit life. Beneath the commandments, however, is the theological outrage: "Sell what you have, yield, submit, follow."

Such a glimpse into evangelical radicalness makes the commandments less severe, easier to embrace, but less important. The commandments are not rejected; but we may move beyond them to a more intense, more joyous obedience. The hard issue is to move beyond self and our precious integrity to the restlessness that undermines and heals. Job's terrible virtue attempted to keep life together in God's absence. God, however, as the poet knew, is present, undomesticated, unencumbered, capable of awe in savage freedom. It is God's lack of domestication that frees us from the little traps of scruple that we mistake for the kingdom. We, like Job, are asked, "Where were you?" We may answer like Adam, hidden in our fearful disobedience, or, like Job, hiding in our fearful obedience. Where were you? Perchance at praise, yielding, being freed, healed, and astonished by a different life. Our new speech of praise lets us join the choir of glad delight. Such new speech makes obedience more dangerous and more daring.

CHAPTER 12
Trusting in the Water-Food-Oil Supply

Psalm 23

A Psalm of David

>The Lord is my shepherd, I shall not want.
>   He makes me lie down in green pastures;
>he leads me beside still waters;
>   he restores my soul.
>He leads me in right paths
>   for his name's sake.
>Even though I walk through the darkest valley,
>   I fear no evil;
>for you are with me;
>   your rod and your staff—
>   they comfort me.
>You prepare a table before me
>   in the presence of my enemies;
>you anoint my head with oil;
>   my cup overflows.
>Surely goodness and mercy shall follow me
>   all the days of my life,
>and I shall dwell in the house of the Lord
>   my whole life long.

Texts: Psalm 23
John 9:1-41

L ent is a special season in the life of the church. It gives us
    time to pause, to think, to reflect, to decide, to ponder the
    painful life of Jesus, and to see our own life afresh in rela-
tion to his. Lent is countercultural, because it moves against our
busyness, our drive and energy and control. Lent asks us to wait
and to watch and to notice—things we do not do well or easily. The
psalm appointed for today, Psalm 23, is known and much loved by
us. The Twenty-third Psalm seems no match for the work of Lent,
because it seems so sweet and so soft and comforting. But something happens to this psalm if we take it as a script for Lent.

As you know, the psalm begins, "The Lord is my shepherd." The
very first word is "The Lord" or, better, "Yahweh." The first word in
Lenten talk is the peculiar name of the God of Israel, the one who
makes heaven and earth, and who liberates and heals and commands. The psalmist is focused upon this peculiar God and the
memory we have of the ways of this God. And then he says of this
God:

> Yahweh is my shepherd.

To think "shepherd" might suggest an idyllic pastoral scene.

In fact, however, the term *shepherd* is political in the Bible. It
means king, sovereign, lord, authority, the one who directs, to
whom I am answerable, whom I trust and serve. In this simple
opening line, the psalm is clear about the goal and focus, the center
and purpose of life: Yahweh and no other. There is no rival loyalty,

*This sermon was prepared for preaching on the Fourth Sunday in Lent in The
Church of Beatitudes in Phoenix; due to illness, it was never preached.*

no competing claim—not economic or political, not liberal or conservative, not sexist or racist, nor any of the other petty loyalties that seduce us. It is a mark of discernment and maturity to strip life down to one compelling loyalty, to be freed of all the others that turn out to be idolatrous.

Then the poet draws a stunning conclusion from this statement about God:

> I shall not want.

I shall not lack anything. I shall not have any other yearnings or desires that fall outside the gifts of God. What God gives will be enough for me. This is a statement of enormous confidence in the generosity of God, the one who knows what we need and gives well beyond all that we ask or think. But notice at the same time that this phrase, "I shall not want," is a decision made against the greed and lust and satiation and aggressive ambition of a consumer society. Our consumer society is driven by the notion that we always must want one more thing, and we are entitled to it, and we will have it no matter what.

And now comes this Lenten invitation: I will refocus my desire. I will not entertain all those other lusts and greeds and yearnings that keep me busy and make me selfish and cause me not to notice my neighbor. Here, I suggest, is a Lenten project for all of us who are competent and affluent and driven and anxious and greedy. Faith in this God requires a refocus of all our desires, because most of our wants are contrived and imagined and phony. This Lord will be Lord of our wants and our needs, and we need much less when we are clear about the wonder and goodness of God. No substitutes allowed or required.

To unpack this statement of focused trust, the poem invites us to two images. The first is this: Imagine that you are a sheep. As you may know, sheep are really dumb. They do not know how to take care of themselves or even to come in out of the rain. Left to their own devices, they would soon be in trouble, hurt, and likely destroyed. A sheep needs a shepherd, and must learn to trust its life to the shepherd. But it matters a lot what kind of shepherd a sheep is able to have. There are all kinds, some good, some bad.

Then this sheep, according to the poet, says, Let me tell you about my shepherd, like whom there is no other. Yahweh, the maker of heaven and earth, the liberator of Israel, is my shepherd whom I trust completely. Let me tell you specifically about why I trust so completely.

This reliable, strong, generous shepherd has done three things for us sheep:

- He has *led us into green pastures*. He has sought out the best grazing ground, so we have plenty to eat. Without such a shepherd, we might have gone hungry on thin pasture lands.
- He has *led us beside still waters*. He has found gentle streams of fresh water where we can drink. Without such gentle streams, we might try fast, rushing streams, and be swept away to our death.
- He has *led us in the paths of righteousness*, which means safe, straight paths. There are dangerous paths on which the sheep may walk in treachery, crooked and narrow and stony, or through dark places where wild animals lurk. But we have been safe.

Indeed this good shepherd has given all that is needed—good food, good water, good paths. What else could an average sheep need? Notice that all the verbs of action are for the shepherd. The sheep has no verbs. The sheep does nothing. The sheep waits and receives and enjoys the gifts. Because the shepherd is generous, the sheep lives a safe, trust-filled life, surrounded by generosity. No hunger, no thirst, no fear, no anxiety, no danger. "All is well," because there is one shepherd who is trusted.

The poem shifts abruptly to a second metaphor. Now it is the image of a traveler going through dangerous territory. Remember, this ancient terrain is not all superhighway and police patrolled. It is more like the man with the Good Samaritan who went on a journey and got mugged (Luke 10:30). The journey is one pervaded by threat and danger.

But remember, Yahweh is my shepherd. Yahweh is my guardian and protector. In the most dangerous place, "I fear no evil." This traveler has confidence, even in ominous places, because the travel is accompanied. "Thou art with me." It is precisely the reality of God who is the antidote to our consuming anxiety. The poet has discovered that things on the journey are not as they seem when God is present. We are safer, more cared for then we imagined. It is the presence of God that transforms dangerous places and tough circumstances.

So, says the psalmist, let me tell you about the valley of the shadow of death, when God is present:

- there, on the journey, we are comforted by *God's protective rod and staff*, instruments of guidance. We are not on our own, but guided, guided by God's presence and God's Torah, safe from all that would rob us of life.
- there, on the journey, we thought there were no resources, but in the very presence of need, fear, and hunger, *God sets a table of generous food*. It is like coming around the corner of deep threat, and there in the middle of the road a lavish table of marvelous food, water from the rock, bread from heaven.
- there, on the journey, where we thought there was only scarcity, the God of generosity *pours out precious oil* on our heads, into our cup. Our lives brim over because of God's inexplicable generosity, just where we thought God had no gifts to give.

The journey, with the power and purpose of God, changes the circumstances in which we live. Wilderness becomes home, isolation becomes companionship, scarcity becomes generosity. That is how the life of faith is. It is, to be sure, very different from the life where Yahweh is not at its core.

The poem concludes with two affirmations.

First, "goodness and mercy pursue me." God's friendliness and kindness will run after me and chase me down, grab me and hold me. The verb "follow" is a powerful, active verb. We are being chased by God's powerful love. We run from it. We try to escape. We fear that goodness, because then we are no longer in control. We do not trust such a generosity, and we think our own best efforts are better than God's mercy.

Lent is a time to quit running, to let ourselves be caught and embraced in love, like that of a sheep with safe pasture, like a traveler with rich and unexpected food. Our life is not willed by God to be an endless anxiety. It is, rather, meant to be an embrace, but that entails being caught by God.

The second concluding line is, "I will dwell in the house of the Lord forever," that is, "my whole life long." I will hang around the church. Or I will live in attentive communion with God. I will not depart from the premises of God's life, because I have no desire for a life apart from God. Why would I want to leave? Now, you may think such a conclusion is sweet and unreal, or at least something only for old, tired people who don't get around much anymore.

To the contrary. This conclusion is the reflection of a mature life, when one "comes down where you ought to be." The last line of the psalm asserts that the true joy and purpose of life are to love God and be loved by God, no longer alone, but in communion. Our anti-Lent society gives us many desires—for safety, security, money, power, prestige, excitement, sex, bigger house, better shoes, finer stereo. . . . These, however, will never constitute a good life. The matter has been settled in the first line for this poet. This sheep-community trusts this god and wants nothing else.

You already know this psalm well. There is nothing soft or sweet or easy or sentimental here. This is the voice of a reorganized, refocused, reoriented life. Such a refocus means to see differently, to trust differently, and to obey differently.

The Gospel reading is a long story about a blind boy. Or so it seems, until you pay attention. As you read the story, you see that the real issue is not the blind boy, but his opponents, the Pharisees. They think they know everything and control everything. Jesus, in an enigmatic statement, says to them at the end of the narrative, "Those who do see may become blind." And they answer, "Surely we are not blind, are we?" At the end of the story, it is they who are blind, not the boy. They are blind because they see wrongly. They see only through their control, their arrogance, their meanness, their anxiety. But they miss everything.

Lent is about noticing our blindness and seeing differently. I invite you in this Lent to see differently, maybe even for the first time. To see past your anxiety, your greed, your fear, your control. See yourself as the sheep of this good shepherd, as the traveler in God's good valley, as the citizen at home in God's good house. You will, when you see truly, be free and joyous and generous, unencumbered and grateful. Desire one thing: God's presence. And you will be less driven by all those phony desires that matter not at all.

CHAPTER 13

Deep Waters

Psalm 69:2, 13-15

I sink in deep mire,
where there is no foothold;
I have come into deep waters,
and the flood sweeps over me.

But as for me, my prayer is to you, O LORD.
At an acceptable time, O God,
in the abundance of your steadfast love,
answer me.
With your faithful help rescue me
from sinking in the mire;
let me be delivered from my enemies
and from the deep waters.
Do not let the flood sweep over me,
or the deep swallow me up,
or the Pit close its mouth over me.

Text: Psalm 69:2, 14

The voice that speaks in Psalm 69 is a voice of profound faith. Indeed, it is the voice of all our mothers and fathers in faith who have dared to believe and to speak. On this deadly Friday, we are bold to say that the voice which sounds here is the voice of Jesus, walking the last costly measure of obedience. And because it is the voice of the one who has suffered with us and for us, we say also that it is the voice of all our common humanity, sore pressed, but not yet talked out of faith.

I pursue only one theme from the Psalm. In this poem we notice that honest prayer is situated in the midst of deep threat:

> I sink in deep mire,
>   where there is no foothold;
> I have come into *deep waters*,
>   and the flood sweeps over me. . . .
> Rescue me from sinking in the mire,
>   let me be delivered from my enemies
>   and from the *deep waters*.
> Do not let the flood sweep over me,
>   or the deep swallow me up
>   or the Pit close its mouth over me.
>   (vv. 2, 14-15)

This Friday is the day we enter into the deep threat of faith and of life, for we are at risk. We dare imagine that on this day the threat reaches even close to the throne of God for the waters rise very high. So consider the gospel sounding this day in the midst of threat, for it must sound there, if it has any validity at all.

Chapters 13, 14, and 15 were preached at All Saints Episcopal Church, Atlanta. The Episcopal practice for Good Friday consists of an extended service with three homilies. Among the assigned texts for the day is Psalm 69. For these three sermons, I sought to accent different dimensions of the Psalm.

Twice the poet speaks of "deep waters" that are rising and surging. The phrase refers to the primitive, elemental awareness that the dry land of creation is surrounded by the hostile, untamed waters of chaos. Those waters of chaos may subside, but then they come again, fierce and relentless, pounding at the edges of the dry land, laying siege to all our fragile arrangements and our little safe spots of earth, threatening to wash it all away.

The phrase "deep waters" invites us to think large about Good Friday. Too much we have reduced the day to sin and forgiveness, to personal salvation "through the blood." The larger drama enacted is that the power of death is on the loose and does its worst work on this day. That is why in some Gospel accounts, at the death of Jesus, there come earthquake and darkness and disorder. The chaos came for those dread hours because the king is dead, order has failed, and the raw elements of undomesticated chaos surge and laugh in ugly triumph.

We wait in the quiet and the dark to see if chaos will recede, we wait for three long hours. It is for us a time open for stocktaking and for noticing in honesty that the powers of chaos and death are indeed untamed, even among us. We suspect that these powers take advantage of greed and hate and fear in order to do their work. But the power itself is deeper, at the muddy bottom of the river of life.

The prayer of faith arises exactly in the midst of chaos. The chaos comes as the economic order dysfunctions, and the index of unemployment and poverty and homelessness rises. The chaos comes as civility is replaced by terror, brutality, and harassment, and neighbors become victims and perpetrators of violence upon each other. The chaos comes as more and more poison is dumped into our brief earthly nest, poison that is profit driven. The land shrivels, the birds flee, and we do not yet connect greed with cancer. Life, public and broad, personal and intimate, is indeed in jeopardy, always so, but acutely so among us now, poignantly so on this Friday . . . in the deep waters.

What to do in our fearful helplessness as the waters rise? The voice of faith in this psalm brings the chaos into relation with the power of God. The chaos is so much more realistic and palpable than the power of God. The threat we can see, the power of God we can only speak about and trust in. But both times "deep waters" are mentioned, it is in order that God should be addressed, brought to awareness, so that God must enter into the chaos and the chaos may be reshaped by the power of God.

The psalmist prays:

> Save me, O God . . . I have come to *deep waters,*
> In your steadfast love, rescue me from the *deep waters.*
> (vv. 1-2, 13-14)

Under threat, even on Friday, this psalm refuses to host the idea that chaos is limitless. The very act of the prayer is an affirmation that watery chaos has limits, boundaries, and edges, because the waters butt up against the power of God.

On this Friday of chaos, we are not watching simply the unbounded power of chaos savage the earth. We are rather watching chaos push to its extreme limit, doing its worst, most destructive work, and spending itself without finally prevailing. The psalm invites us to honesty about the threat. More than that, however, the psalm is buoyant in its conviction that all around the chaos, guarding its rise, monitoring its threat, is the counterpower of life, only haunting and shadowing, not too soon evident, but abidingly there. This voice of faith acknowledges the chaos, but then submits it to the larger power of God. So Jesus in that supreme moment of threat, does not yield, but announces in evangelical triumph, "It is finished." It is decided! It is accomplished! It is completed in triumph!

So what to do midst the threat? Do what believing Jesus and trusting Jews and Christians have always done. Refuse the silence, reject despair, resist the devastating, debilitating assault of chaos, and speak a counterspeech. This psalm is not simply a passive, pious act of trust in God. It is rather a bold, abrasive speech which addresses God in the imperative, and which, in the utterance of the imperative, puts chaos on notice that we will not yield, will not succumb, will not permit the surging of chaos to define the situation.

The response to the threat in this prayer is twofold, two items closely related, but clearly distinguishable. There is *the hovering, magisterial limit* of God that curbs the threat. And there is *the abrasive, insistent speech of faith* that evokes the limit of God. On this Friday, it is worth asking, as the waters of chaos rise before our very eyes: Do we wait in stunned, awed silence, counting on the power of God to curb? Biblical faith is never in favor of pious silence. It is rather for direct, assertive, insistent demand that refuses to sit silently while the waters rise. I can imagine this man Jesus and this people who have not lost their voice of faith, even on Friday, willing to speak shrilly against the flood, against the hate and the greed, against the poison and the fear and the indignity. For Israel believes that its faithful speech is the earnest and harbinger of God's own majestic intrusion, that God comes into the deep waters at the behest of the faithful who watch in the night and who know that chaos is not normal and must not be docilely accepted.

As I pondered over "deep waters," I heard this other text in which God assures:

> Do not fear, for I have redeemed you;
>   I have called you by name, you are mine.
> When you pass through the waters, I will be with you;
>   and through the river, they shall not overwhelm you.
>   (Isa. 43:1b-2a)

The promise is that God will come to be in the waters with us, submitting to the chaos, and by submitting, transforming the waters. So we dare imagine that Jesus did not die abandoned on Friday. As he submitted to the sweeping, surging waters, his God and parent were present in the chaos, thereby transforming the waters into a place of rescuing communion.

In Martin Scorcese's awesome movie, *Cape Fear*, a family is under assault by a genuinely evil man, an embodiment of evil, a man who has been wronged by the father of the family. As the story unfolds, the man is bent on vengeance. The family seeks to hide out on a riverboat, but their nemesis pursues them even there. There comes an enormous storm as the chaos of the river rises in the movie, and a terrible struggle ensues. The boat is destroyed, the family nearly drowned, the landscape ravished by the deep waters. One can feel the terrible, irresistible power of chaos.

With the last ounce of energy, the family pushes the evil man down into the surging river. He is by this time nearly insane in his rage. As he sinks into the waters, he utters, one more time, a series of savage threats and curses. But just as he sinks finally into the water, his speech changes. One almost misses it. He sings of crossing the Jordan into the land of promise. It is a stunning film rendition of chaos that is primordial. Clearly this is no ordinary river but the power of death. In the last instant, just when death seems to have won, the deep waters are transformed into the rescuing, saving baptizing Jordan River.

This is what we confess on this Friday, the day when death and chaos do their worst. This day is the very moment of God's powerful triumph for life, when creation is reordered for new life. It remains for us to enact this odd metamorphosis. It is precisely on this Friday when God is seen as safe boundary, when hope is known as power to counter chaos, that the very chaos can become a place of new gifts, the locus of trust that becomes a venue for communion. Death becomes a place of saving, and we inch toward Easter.

The world now waits to see whether the faithful church can enter its Friday of chaos, enter in hope and resistance, to trust enough to let the threat become the home of rescue. The transformation requires profound faith and high hutzpah. How dare anyone under such threat say in triumph, "It is finished!"? Such nerve called trust causes the waters to recede, and life in all its fruitfulness may begin again, on Friday toward Sunday.

14
Penultimate Honesty

Psalm 69:19-29

You know the insults I receive,
and my shame and dishonor;
my foes are all known to you.
Insults have broken my heart,
so that I am in despair.
I looked for pity, but there was none;
and for comforters, but I found none.
They gave me poison for food,
and for my thirst they gave me vinegar to drink.
Let their table be a trap for them,
a snare for their allies.
Let their eyes be darkened so that they cannot see,
and make their loins tremble continually.
Pour out your indignation upon them,
and let your burning anger overtake them.
May their camp be a desolation;
let no one live in their tents.
For they persecute those whom you have struck down,
and those whom you have wounded,
they attack still more.
Add guilt to their guilt;
may they have no acquittal from you.
Let them be blotted out of the book of the living;
let them not be enrolled among the righteous.

But I am lowly and in pain;
let your salvation, O God, protect me.

Text: Psalm 69:19-29

The politics of Good Friday are heavy-duty. After all, the authorities are discussing what to do with a figure who seems to be an enemy of the state or, perhaps even more, an enemy of the church. There are in the air hints and whispers of a coup, a new king, even though there is no vacancy in the office. In the gray background hovers Rome, ready like the Soviet Union to rush into Poland or the United States into Nicaragua, if there is excessive unrest. One must be very careful in these delicate defenses of the status quo, for there is little room for maneuverability in an occupied land. I propose that Good Friday is an invitation to ponder this heavy-duty struggle for power, to locate our chosen role in the drama of coup and defense and, finally, a state execution.

The cast of characters in the drama is not only well known, but completely predictable. There is the Roman governor who wants to get by without being noticed. He is not a bad man, mostly a cowardly bureaucrat who wishes that the problem of Jesus would evaporate, because no good can come for him of such unrest. He seems almost sympathetic toward Jesus but will not risk anything. The second major role is played by the venomous crowd of fire-eaters, who are portrayed as too eager, excessively patriotic, insisting upon decisive action, exactly what the governor wants to avoid.

The third character is this innocent, enigmatic Jesus. He is the cause of all the trouble, not for what he does, but for who he is—such a pure, innocent, guileless figure that he embarrasses and exposes all the others as frauds and fakes. While the others posture, Jesus exudes authority of a very different kind, an authority with which the others cannot cope. Both the governor and the crowd are undone and immobilized by the authority of this third character. I invite you to ponder this other kind of authority, which puts the world into turmoil in its frantic attempts to keep this odd power out.

Of these three characters, only this innocent outsider has a psalm for his use. We have no hint that either the governor or the crowd is allowed a psalm; that is, neither of them reaches into the old tradition for a guiding script on how to speak or what to say.

Psalm 69 shows how this counterpower of Jesus conducts itself, as though the political crudities of Rome and Jerusalem really do not count. In this hour, I want to speak about the penultimate power of honesty. The psalm is something of an embarrassment to us, because we do not expect such speech, especially on the lips of Jesus. But Jesus is a child of this Jewish script. He knows that this is how the faithful speak in the face of such a crisis.

It strikes us that this voice of innocence is filled with determined hostility toward his detractors and enemies. The voice of faith under attack sounds like this:

> You know the insults I receive,
>   and my shame and dishonor;
>   my foes are all known to you.
> Insults have broken my heart,
>   so that I am in despair.
> I looked for pity, but there was none;
>   and for comforters, but I found none.
> They gave me poison for food,
>   and for my thirst they gave me vinegar to drink.
>   (vv. 19-21)

The speaker describes the abuse, insults, shame, and dishonor that produces despair. The speaker has been badly maltreated.

Moreover, the speaker wants retaliation from God. This is a determined petition for vengeance, that the abusers should be humiliated, defeated, and destroyed:

> Let their table be a trap for them,
>   a snare for their allies.
> Let their eyes be darkened so that they cannot see,
>   and make their loins tremble continually. . . .
> May their camp be a desolation;
>   let no one live in their tents. . . .

Let them be blotted out of the book of the living;
let them not be enrolled among the righteous.

(vv. 22-28)

Some mouthful! Some mouthful that may sound strange to you on this Holy Friday. But then, I did not pick this psalm. The church chose it long ago for its poignant witness to the reality of Jesus' death.

I submit that this psalm shows that this ominous Friday involves a dispute about the moral quality of reality. The church on this Friday must not let the day become maudlin or romantic or magical or privatistic. So consider these points:

Jesus is a genuinely innocent man who has kept the Torah, and who is entitled to the well-being produced by Torah obedience. This voice of innocence refuses to be cynical about virtue. The one whom we trust this day is the one who had courage, freedom, and imagination to live in the world of real and seductive power, and to live in it according to his uncompromising vocation. This is what made him a threat to the governor and to the crowd. His alternative mode of power rooted in Torah obedience was evident to all who came into contact with him. His goodness contrasts with the shabbiness of those all around him.

In his innocence, Jesus knew, trusted, and expected that the wicked would need to answer for what they did. Thus this prayer for vengeance is not venom on the part of Jesus. It is simply an affirmation and an insistence that evil has its own painful reward that cannot be avoided. These people should indeed get what they have coming to them, because God has ordered the world in morally uncompromising ways. No softness here!

The enemies of Jesus have not guarded his dignity nor enhanced his well-being. They have not taken seriously that human beings are entitled to respect simply because they exist. They had done a quick assessment of Jesus and found him to be powerless by their standards, politically unimportant, and therefore one to be abused with impunity. But they misread, because they had not taken into account his moral authority that gave him another kind of power, that put him well beyond their intimidation, coercion, and manipulation. They miscalculated about him, and about the God who stood near to him. This psalm has no doubt that their crass forms of power that abuse and diminish finally cannot prevail.

The juxtaposition of Jesus' innocence and his petition for vengeance requires utter honesty to describe social relations that are abusive and exploitative. The reason there is such a showdown is that Jesus turns out to be a truth-speaker in a society of massive and pervasive distortion. We have made Jesus too pious, too nice, too patient, too polite. He was none of these. His was a dangerous alternative kind of power that was prepared to name names and to describe social relations exactly as they were. In the life of Jesus, it is clear that all the raw, abusive power in the world could not prevail. The honesty of Jesus is grounded in his confidence about the rule of God.

All of this drama of innocence, vengeance, and honesty is kicked upstairs, uttered to God in prayer. That is, Jesus is not simply doing social analysis. Jesus is practicing faith that joins together honest social criticism and profound confidence in God. By turning this heavy-duty political conflict into a prayer, Jesus raises the stakes by surfacing the large question of theodicy.

"Theodicy" is a big word for the question, Do we live in a just world? Do we live in a world that is morally coherent and reliable, where virtue counts, where obedience matters, where care and compassion make a difference? Or do we live in a world where only raw force finally counts, and virtue is silly and romantic?

So what is it that happened in that drama of power on that Friday? Do not give up the question for a heavenly, transcendental transaction out beyond worldly reality, for these are real people struggling over real power. Friday is the ultimate day in which the church asks with unblinking honesty about the moral quality of reality. Or is it just that money talks and might makes right?

There is ample ground for cynicism. The rich get richer, the powerful grow more ugly and cynical, and nice guys finish last. A public officer who prattles about the goodness of the "private sector" acting for the poor in place of the government puts down fourteen dollars on his tax return for charity. Big nations, including the United States, march against little ones whenever they want. Tax laws favor the powerful and the well-connected, and the federal government becomes a cynical meeting place for the wealthy, because the market economy has overcome the reality and requirements of the social fabric.

The reality of Good Friday, as the governor and the crowd learned only late, is an occasion for dangerous social criticism. There is an insistence in the life of Jesus that innocence gives power, that inhumanity is not a safe policy, that honesty is required of reality, and that things must be called by their right names. It matters enormously whether power disputes are handled in the context of unaccommodating moral reality. Jesus got himself killed because he exposed the false ordering of power that paid no attention to the little ones, among whom he counted himself. He answered the powerbrokers sharply and defiantly, even as he prayed for them:

> You have no power over me,
> unless it had been given you from above.
> (John 19:11)

Jesus has become for us the lens through which we reread power, social relations, and formal policies. Jesus stands alongside all the powerless in his abrasive prayer, demanding justice on earth from God. Jesus' innocence is an exposé of and a threat to every other kind of power. It would indeed be quite an Easter if the church resolved to come clean on this moral claim. Talk about a coup! No wonder Jesus made the governor nervous and the crowd frantic. They killed him, but he kept praying in his dangerous, abrasive honesty. The prayer he prays insists that God will not be mocked,

> For the Lord hears the needy,
> and does not despise his own that are in bonds.
>
> (v. 33)

15

Beyond Honesty to Trust

Psalm 69:13-14a, 16-18, 33

But as for me, my prayer is to you, O LORD.
  At an acceptable time, O God,
  in the abundance of your steadfast love,
    answer me.
With your faithful help rescue me
  from sinking in the mire.

Answer me, O LORD, for your steadfast love is good;
  according to your abundant mercy, turn to me.
Do not hide your face from your servant,
  for I am in distress—make haste to answer me.
Draw near to me, redeem me,
  set me free because of my enemies.

For the LORD hears the needy,
  and does not despise his own that are in bonds.

Text: Psalm 69:13-14a, 16-18, 33

In Psalm 69 "Friday faith" moves beyond itself. The poet speaks out of the deep waters of chaos that are unloosed to death and looks the deep waters full in the face. The poet speaks with a sense of outrage, out of innocence that is not honored, for abuse and oppression seem to prevail. In outrage not unlike that of Job, the speaker dwells on his own innocence and the need for retaliation from God. But on Friday, this voice of faith does not dwell on the threat of the waters nor on the failure of innocence. Finally, the speaker is able to get his mind and voice off himself, to turn his anxious, threatened life over to God. This is no small matter, for when we are threatened and abused we tend to dwell on our sorry condition. Faith, however, moves past self-pity to the God who can make a difference.

At the core of this Friday faith, there is a turn from self to God, from trouble to hope. At the center of the drama of Friday, the crucified one turns from self in an act of confident self-abandonment. The news offered us, which I announce to you, is that the only way from Friday to Sunday, from threat to new life, is to entrust one's self and one's world to this God who is in, with, and under the deep waters.

So the psalmist, after a massive complaint, turns the rhetoric:

> As for me, my prayer is to you, O Lord. (v. 13a)

The *me* is turned over to the *you*. There is another one who is the key player in our life. This wondrous phrase of turning suggests three important matters to us.

First, there is hope and possibility because of the capacity and readiness to say "you, thou," an agent other than myself. Our society suffers from the deep, mistaken conviction that "I" am the center of my existence, that God has no hands but ours, that if you want anything done, you must do it for yourself. But this *Thou* now addressed and acknowledged is an actor, an agent, a rescuer who can be summoned and mobilized into the center of trouble, into the threat of Friday.

Second, the statement "from me to thou" is an act of prayer. We take prayer so easily and routinely, but we should notice what a bold, revolutionary act this prayer is. Prayer is not pious abdication. It is a daring maneuver whereby the speaker breaks the categories of trouble and shatters the closed world of threat. It is a defiant alternative to sinking into the deep waters. In a world where there is only me, prayer is a nervy act of insistence that makes no sense. The only people who can do the daring act of prayer are those who know that the world is visited, attended to, and occupied by our advocate who can overpower death.

Third, the prayer names the one addressed, "O Yahweh." In this utterance of the name, the speaker appeals to the whole Jewish memory of liberation. The one summoned in this moment is the God who formed the world and liberated the slaves, who gave the land and attended to the poor who needed a safe place. Prayer of this sort is not a private deal, but is an act that reclaims and reasserts the whole of this trusting, grateful community. The God of creation and liberation is the one who intrudes upon Friday to create new possibility.

Then the prayer makes a second statement of great trust:

> At an acceptable time, O God, answer. (v. 13b)

What it cost to say "acceptable time"! Acceptable to whom? We might have expected franticness and urgency: Save me and do it now, or else I will die.

But so confident and trusting is the speaker that the issue is not forced. While Friday seems short and death seems near, the timetable of rescue is left to God. We watch the sun go down on Friday, and the body of Jesus has expired. We wait through the long Saturday and it seems too late. Nonetheless, "at your acceptable time" is not rushed. It turns out that the acceptable time is Sunday. The acceptable time when God hears and answers and rescues is Easter.

In the meantime, the voice of faith prepares to wait. Do you remember the cadences of the speech of Martin Luther King, Jr., in his rhetoric of hope?

> How long till freedom . . . not long;
> How long till justice . . . not long;
> How long till dignity . . . not long;
> How long . . . not long, not long, not long.

Why not long? Because God presides over the times, and the waiting of the faithful is trusting time. George Steiner concludes his book on faith, *Real Presences*, saying that pain and hope and "flesh which tastes of ash and of spirit . . . are always Sabbatarian," that is, always pivot on the long wait of Saturday (p. 232). It is this "immensity of waiting" that belongs to humanity, and for that we can only be patient. The faithful are patient and confident through Saturday, because the God who lasted through Friday is the God who acts in an acceptable time.

But the waiting we do in faith is not endlessly patient. There is with the hope and waiting, an insistence addressed to God. The poet says three times in an imperative:

> In the abundance of your steadfast love, *answer me.* (v. 13)
> *Answer me*, O Lord, for your steadfast love is good. (v. 16)
> I am in distress . . . make haste to *answer me.* (v. 17)

The tone is like a little child, growing impatient about an adult who tarries too long. And when the asking of the child is ignored, he becomes louder, more shrill, and more demanding. He tugs at your sleeve and is convinced that the time is short and there must now be a serious and intentional response. The speaker, in innocence, is entitled to attentiveness and claims it as a right. So the child says insistently, "Look at me, answer me, now."

What courage and nerve, to believe that "deep waters" is a place for petition and conversation, to trust that the answering involvement of Yahweh will decisively change the situation and alter the threat. God is enough. The real terror of Friday is that God is not there: "My God, My God, why have you forsaken me, abandoned me?" But God can come and God will come, with power, with healing:

> Do not fear, for *I am with you*,
> 　　Do not be afraid, for I am your God.
> Though I walk through the valley of the
> 　　shadow of death,
> I will not fear, for *you are with me.*

"With me" in power, in fidelity, in mercy, in attentiveness, with me, so I am unafraid.

Two times, the petition of this psalm utters the deepest word of our faith:

> In your abundant *steadfast love*, answer me (v. 13).
> Answer me, O Yahweh, for your *steadfast love* is good (v. 16).

The prayer centers in the double use of "steadfast love, " reinforced by the term "faithful help" (v. 13). "Steadfast love" entails a loyal commitment of solidarity that is larger than reality, stronger than death, deeper than the deep waters. Steadfast love means to be protectively and safely surrounded by the resilient *Thou* of God.

The prayer is a response of faith to the promise and vow of God, that God will stand in solidarity, that God's fidelity is not interrupted, even by the threat of death, even by the rising of deep waters, even by the dread of crucifixion. So we ponder this commitment from God that the world can hardly entertain:

> I am sure that neither life, nor death, nor angels, nor principalities,
> nor things present, nor things to come, nor powers, nor heights, nor

depths, nor anything else in all creation, can separate us from the love of God in Christ Jesus our Lord.

(Rom. 8:38-39)

Nothing in all creation—not even Friday!!

That is a word people like us may cherish, but we also tremble over it. We cherish it, because it assures us that in the deepest, most dangerous drama of our life there is an assurance beyond assault. We tremble over it, however, precisely because we are not romantic. We do not lightly make claims that fly in the face of so much evidence to the contrary. So now we are at the Friday of the Holocaust, of Hiroshima and napalm, the babies in Romania, the blacks in South Africa, the street people in Atlanta, and the deep despairs and hard deaths about which we all know so intimately. We are at countless Fridays that admit of no easy resolution. And we tremble with the verdict, "We had hoped this one was the one to redeem." We had hoped, but alas!

So I speak a wondrous word to you, that the cosmic intention of fidelity does not wince, even on Friday. In the most bereft places of your life and of our common life, there is this passion for being with us. But this wondrous word is spoken to you now on Friday, and therefore spoken with some unease, not triumphant, not gloating, but sure.

So imagine the whole world gathered on this dense Friday. The world wants from us honesty, honesty enough to say that ours is a world not yet made right. In the midst of honesty, the world also expects from us trust, daring affirmations that do not escape Friday, but which imagine that the most ominous Fridays are nevertheless in the realm of God's fidelity.

We face two temptations: One is to rush to Sunday and have it all joyous. The other is to settle in cynicism and take up residence in a permanent, hopeless Saturday.

Our work is neither of these, but bold prayer, trusting God's time to be full for us, full of mercy, full of steadfast love, full of counterpower for life. We hope for the world on this Friday that which the world, in its staggered condition, cannot hope for itself, the truth of steadfastness resolved even against chaos.

16 What You Eat Is What You Get

Proverbs 15:17

*Better is a dinner of vegetables where love is
than a fatted ox and hatred with it.*

Texts: Proverbs 15:17; Mark 8:14-21; Luke 14:15-24

W hat you eat is what you get! At the first table is gravy
and roast beef and rice. This is the main course, but
there have been preliminary courses of soup, clam
chowder, after hors d'oeuvres; and there will be a rich dessert and
nuts and fruit and claret. At the center, between soup and nuts, is
roast beef, large, rare slices—call it fatted ox. You can kill a fatted ox
for a special party. But these people have it every night. Every
night—extravagance and satiation, and with it pressure and anxiety. They have eaten this way so long they do not regard their eating
as conspicuous consumption. They simply enjoy fatted ox. They
can afford it. They can afford everything, so why not?

*This sermon was preached during a summer session at Columbia Theological
Seminary.*

In describing the scene, the wisdom teacher construes what else goes with such eating. Maybe there is such a regular rich diet with freedom and ease. The wisdom teacher, however, imagines that such a diet bespeaks busyness and overextendedness, drivenness, restlessness, and anxiety. To have such food, you have to keep at things all the time—drive, drive, drive, great second effort—and then be satiated. After a while such extravagance is not very special, not even noticed, and not much appreciated.

Worse than that, it takes two incomes to maintain the menu and everything that goes with it: Two incomes, a busy schedule, a crowded social calendar, long hours (not just for roast beef, but all the things along with it, of social expectation and entertainment), stopping at the store, rushing home, fixing, too many evening meetings, cook it, eat it, three phone calls, a good dinner with little time to eat it. The kids just home from soccer and off to band, what a waste, too much on edge, driven to stay in place, "jonesing." They do not know how good they have it, the kids, unappreciative, ungrateful, demanding. Maybe roast beef need not lead to all of that. The wisdom teacher summarizes his view:

Fatted ox and strife with it.

The roast beef becomes a cipher for excessive, luxurious living, the social requirements and tensions, excessive preoccupation with things that lead to tension, quarreling, fear, and hate. "No, I won't be home; I'm not really that hungry. Feed it to the dog."

What you eat is what you get. There is another table set for us. Not much on it, only greens, call it herbs. Just simple vegetables, a little bread, plain wine, quiet, simplicity, no leftovers, no fuss. Call it health food, but don't romanticize. Call it poor people's food. A dinner of herbs—greens—is a virtue once, but every night makes it seem like an unending Lent.

It is all we can afford. Well, that is because you don't work very hard or very much and are not productive. You could work in the afternoons and afford some meat regularly. But a choice has been made: work less, more time to do what we want. More time for each other. The whole afternoon to read and think, to be with the kids, special time unhurried for their things. We arrive at supper unrushed, without great food. We eat slowly or it will be over too soon, not much food. But time for what there is. Maybe the neighbors will be there, or we eat early and go to choir or to the peace rally, but before we do, sharing and laughing and listening, just listening—and peace, before the peace rally. We finish, nourished, not excessively full, but hunger done, and healing comes. It is not just the food, because the difference between spinach and beef does not amount to much, except that the two epitomize a whole range of choices for people and things, for ease or drivenness, for sufficiency and satiation, for listening and bickering, contentment gained not by consuming but by communion. The wisdom teacher said it this way: "A dinner of herbs where love is."

Spinach breeds love no more than beef yields hate. The proverb only imagines two ways in the world, one that moves from well-being to caring, the other that moves from franticness to having and gaining the whole world and finishing supper with a diminished soul. Soulless food causes loss of soul.

We are in process, always in process, of deciding what's for dinner, because what you eat is what you get. We are always deciding about when to eat and who is invited and how much we need and what else we do not need. We do know that the quality of our diet is not unrelated to love and hate, to joy and fear, to delight and resentment, because how we eat is how we live. The proverb seems such a simple observation about eating; it turns out to be a summons about the gospel, by way of our eating habits, and the large crisis of a "food disorder."

It could be that there is something merely *nostalgic* in this sapiential contrast, of wishing for simpler days unencumbered by modernity, affluence, and the rat race. It could be this is romanticizing that when folks had less they cared more. It could be that in Israel they noticed Solomon's rich table had caused new waves of hostility and oppression (1 Kings 4:22-28). You know how the line goes. There was a time when we had less, but more time and more talk. We were not always having something broken to be repaired, because we had less. We lived more "hands on" before we were smitten with self-indulgence and comfort. This may be only nostalgia, for perhaps there never were good old days or, if there were, we cannot simply remove ourselves from our present life of urgency and business. I may be exhausted, but I cannot walk away from it.

It may be that the wisdom teachers yearned for the good old days. Or perhaps there is something here about *eschatology*, about the long-term promises of God for how things will finally be. Perhaps the shift from ox to herb, from beef to greens, is an anticipation of the kingdom that comes among us. We know enough about cattle and grassland and what it takes to produce a cow that we cannot all be at the table with equality at a high standard of living. The ones who have beef must take food away from others. There is not enough grassland, and so the powerful act like the Corinthians, eating meat and crowding at the table while others look on in hunger and poverty. The promised kingdom of God which is to come will have all equal, with enough to eat, perhaps only greens, healthy, unrushed, unhurried, time to listen and to care and to laugh and to look and to notice. The promised table of the kingdom is not dulling satiation, but enough food to sustain us in joy and in sorrow together, more cared for and so eating less. It is not a banquet for the rich and extravagant, but for all—healed, valued, at peace, no drivenness, no disruptive phone calls. Everyone is there, and all there are important.

We live between the *nostalgia* of what might have been, and a *promise* of what will surely be, when all are invited, the poor, the maimed, the blind, the lame, the unacceptable, and us. All are welcomed, all at peace, all rejoicing, all loved, all fed, and just greens.

The wisdom teachers dare to assert that one of these meals is better than the other. There are choices to be made about diet, and one choice is not as good as another. Maybe we will conclude that herbs are not better than ox. In the world of social reality, however, what the proverb knows is that you cannot have only herbs or only ox. You get a whole world with each food, because food is a social reality in a social context. You cannot have just herbs or ox. You will get beef and strife, or greens and love, because what you eat is what you get. In choosing food we choose our style, our context, and our company, and our way in the world. In selecting our food, we act out our hopes and our yearnings. We tilt our life toward some satisfaction. One is better than the other—herbs with love, ox with strife—because herbs with love lets us be who we in fact are, lets us live as God would have us live, lets us be who we most yearn to be, in peace, safe, in love.

The choices of ox and herbs, of greens and beef, of love or strife, are not little family choices made in private when you go into the kitchen. They are big, far-ranging public choices concerning foreign policy and budget and land reform and dreams. We do not pick our food just before dinner. We pick our food by how we value life, and how we build policy and how we shape law, and how we arrange money, and how we permit poverty and hunger in a land of abundance. The proverb might envision life in the palace with too much meat, and the peasants with none. Perhaps the proverb is a picture of the wealthy man and Lazarus, or of wealthy North Americans overfed and Latin Americans at risk without land. Perhaps the image is of empty tables in the dust of Soweto and luxury stores in Johannesburg, perhaps of kosher affluence in Jerusalem and empty rice bowls in the Gaza Strip. We choose our food and we choose our life. We sit at the table, somewhere between nostalgia for the good old days and hope for what God has promised, somewhere between what might have been and what will surely be. And we make a choice. Mostly we choose our future not with our minds thinking clearly, but with our stomachs and appetites and ambitions, making or not making time to care, or time to love, or time for strife.

Listen to an exposition of the proverb in the teaching of Jesus:

Now they had forgotten to bring bread; and they had only one loaf
with them in the boat. And he cautioned them, saying, "Take heed,
beware of the leaven of the Pharisees and the leaven of Herod." And
they discussed it with one another, saying, "We have no bread."
And being aware of it, Jesus said to them, "Why do you discuss the
fact that you have no bread? Do you not yet perceive or
understand? Are your hearts hardened? Having eyes do you not see,
and having ears do you not hear? And do you not remember?
When I broke the five loaves for the five thousand, how many baskets full of broken pieces did you take up?" They said to him,
"Twelve." "And the seven for the four thousand, how many baskets
full of broken pieces did you take up?" And they said to him,
"Seven." And he said to them, "Do you not yet understand?"
(Mark 8:14-21)

The wisdom teacher said with conviction and simplicity:

Better is a dinner with herbs where love is,
than a fatted ox and hatred with it.

Jesus said wistfully, and with some impatience:

Do you not yet understand about the bread?

Then he added enigmatically:

Blessed are you that hunger now,
for you shall be satisfied.
(Luke 6:21)

17

Always Again Before Nebuchadnezzar

Daniel 3:14-20

Nebuchadnezzar said to them, "Is it true, O Shadrach, Meshach, and Abednego, that you do not serve my gods and you do not worship the golden statue that I have set up? Now if you are ready when you hear the sound of the horn, pipe, lyre, trigon, harp, drum, and entire musical ensemble to fall down and worship the statue that I have made, well and good. But if you do not worship, you shall immediately be thrown into a furnace of blazing fire, and who is the god that will deliver you out of my hands?"

Shadrach, Meshach, and Abednego answered the king, "O Nebuchadnezzar, we have no need to present a defense to you in this matter. If our God whom we serve is able to deliver us from the furnace of blazing fire and out of your hand, O king, let him deliver us. But if not, be it known to you, O king, that we will not serve your gods and we will not worship the golden statue that you have set up."

Then Nebuchadnezzar was so filled with rage against Shadrach, Meshach, and Abednego that his face was distorted. He ordered the furnace heated up seven times more than was customary, and ordered some of the strongest guards in his army to bind Shadrach, Meshach, and Abednego and to throw them into the furnace of blazing fire.

Texts: Daniel 3:14-20
John 8:31-42

Nebuchadnezzar is the only superpower left. He proposes a "new world order." He imagines himself at the center of that new order, ready to impose his purpose by every coercive means necessary. Such a superpower can do a lot of good. Such an order will work all right—except for this odd community of believers that has a First Commandment in its craw, this odd rule of exclusivity that precludes signing on for any other loyalty. This community, embodied by Shadrach and his friends, has ringing in it ears, "Thou shalt have no other God." The text we have sets up a deep conflict between imposed order and the claim of the Exodus God who intends freedom for Israel from every such imposed power.

The story is shaped in three predictable scenes. In the first scene, we have only the decree of Nebuchadnezzar (vv. 13-15). The king is the only one who speaks. He is already at the beginning "in a furious rage," because he has a premonition that these emancipated Jews will not submit to his yoke or to his authority. Any self-respecting superpower will require that the subjects "fall down and worship the statue," that is, give visible, bodily consent to the imposed order. Do it in worship, so that the empire may be wrapped in a flag of religious legitimacy. The mesmerizing music of the empire begins—horn, pipe, drum, harp, the whole orchestra, the offering

This sermon was preached at the National Cathedral in Washington. The readings, in the Episcopal order, are for the saint-day of William Augustus Muhlenberg, whose own life witnessed against the dangers of self-sufficiency and indifference. Muhlenberg was a German Lutheran who became an Episcopal priest. Born in 1796, his ministry in New York focused on evangelism, beauty in worship, and an egalitarian sense of the church's response to the needs of society.

of stupefying Musak™, to make the allegiance less painful. The music of the empire is an invitation to give up your identity and your vocation in order to have a little peace. Nebuchadnezzar is always giving the signal for such music, an invitation to succumb in mindless, abdicating docility. The faithful, loyal, self-conscious Jews are asked to become abdicating, succumbing subjects.

In the second scene, the three men of faith, Shadrach, Meshach, and Abednego, are models of resistance (vv. 16-18). Because they have said a firm yes to their faith, they must say no to the false control of their lives that Nebuchadnezzar seeks to impose. The three must refuse liturgic assent, because their lives belong, in irreversible ways, to another loyalty, and their bodies are aimed at a different faith.

Their act of resistance is stark and unambiguous. There is no vacillation in their attitude, no negotiation, no tentativeness. Just simple clarity. "We refuse your authority. We have no need to give you an answer. We will not enter into your discourse; we will not let you define the rules of the game nor the focus of our life."

The reason for such passionate, daring resistance is their confidence in God. They are utterly sure of God's protective presence. "We risk the assurance that God is able to deliver us from your furnace." The faithful do not succumb, because they have a more powerful advocate. That is always the ground for resistance, a ground that Nebuchadnezzar cannot refute.

But then, as if that were not enough, our three fathers in faith utter a second assertion that is stunning in its stubborn candor. "If our God is not able to deliver us from your worst threats, we still will not submit." The three friends make two very different responses. The first response counts on the triumphant power of God. The second allows that God may not be able to stand against the power of Nebuchadnezzar. The three entertain, even in their theological passion, a moment of political realism. "Nonetheless, God with power or not, we will not submit." The First Commandment against other loyalties counts, even if the God of the First Commandment is not very strong. The second ground for resistance is astonishing and gives us pause. It is based, not on God's wondrous, reassuring power, but on a resolve of an identity that will stay with the God of the gospel, no matter what may come.

This second answer leaves Nebuchadnezzar without recourse in the third scene, in which he is again the key actor (vv. 18-20). How could you answer such a defiant statement? Of course the king can make no answer. Instead, Nebuchadnezzar cranks up a new level of rage, as raw power always does when it is pushed into a corner. The king heats up the furnaces of intimidation, seven times more than usual—I mean *hot*! The three resisters are thrust into the persuasive flames that raw power keeps always ready at hand.

And then the reading stops! Nebuchadnezzar thinks he has won. And we will not know the outcome of this unequal context, until the next reading. Of course, it is like that for the faithful when they resist, not knowing the outcome, but refusing nonetheless to answer or submit.

This text has nothing to do with us—except that we are in Lent. This text suggests that Lent is not for cowards. It is for active believers who understand that we are called to resistance against the "rulers of this age" who want to talk us out of our vision, our passion, and our identity. This text has us imagine that we are always before a superpower who will talk us out of our faith. But here are our ancestors, enacting their dangerous, defiant Lent, refusing to succumb or to abdicate their passion for obedience.

Take this drama of liberated resistance in four ways:

1. In the Gospel reading Jesus debates with his fellow Jews. It is an in-house debate about tradition, about father Abraham and the gift of freedom. Jesus insists that freedom comes only from truth-

telling that he himself embodies. The gospel, however, is too dangerous, too stark, too extreme; so his opponents prefer to find comfort in a tradition that is closed, which in their reading yields no dangerous freedom. This particular Jesus is in continuity with the Daniel narrative: Jesus means freedom!

2. To take Nebuchadnezzar as a superpower of course suggests, to you as it does to me, the prideful posturing of the United States, with its military capacity and its economic privilege, stalking the earth, seizing, exploiting, and consuming whatever it wants. We are enmeshed as beneficiaries of this superpower. There is a recurring practice of consumerism and militarism, and when the pipes and drums of our economy play, we fall down in complicity against such an easy practice; yet here is Shadrach, refusing complicity, posing an issue for us in Lent.

3. The superpower may not be Nebuchadnezzar or the United States, or anything so big and visible. Take the image quite intimately and personally: an old defeated self, an addiction, a supermom, a superdad, a superteacher, a superbishop, a supervestry, who starts the music and wants you to "bow down." You struggle when the music begins, tempted to bow down. You struggle for the freedom of the gospel, in order to resist, to reclaim your true self in freedom, no longer conforming, or abdicating, or succumbing. You notice the heat as you resist the temptation; the heat feels oddly like a hot oven.

4. Or finally, this day of William August Muhlenberg: He understood about succumbing to self-sufficiency and indifference and not noticing. He prayed for vision and the capacity to notice the homeless and the destitute. His prayer is an act of resistance for the freedom of the gospel. His prayer is as contemporary as today, because our location in the world has not changed much.

Take this Daniel text for the day. Let your life be shaped for an instant around resistance to the powers that will destroy your freedom and shrivel your life. Notice that the fires can be risked for the sake of freedom. And then, as you ponder, ask, might you be Nebuchadnezzar to someone else?

FOUR

Texts from the New Testament

with Old Testament Allusions

CHAPTER 18
Checkpoint John

Matthew 3:1-12

In those days John the Baptist appeared in the wilderness of Judea, proclaiming, "Repent, for the kingdom of heaven has come near." This is the one of whom the prophet Isaiah spoke when he said,

> *"The voice of one crying out in the wilderness:*
> *'Prepare the way of the Lord,*
> *make his paths straight.'"*

Now John wore clothing of camel's hair with a leather belt around his waist, and his food was locusts and wild honey. Then the people of Jerusalem and all Judea were going out to him, and all the region along the Jordan, and they were baptized by him in the river Jordan, confessing their sins.

But when he saw many Pharisees and Sadducees coming for baptism, he said to them, "You brood of vipers! Who warned you to flee from the wrath to come? Bear fruit worthy of repentance. Do not presume to say to yourselves, 'We have Abraham as our ancestor'; for I tell you, God is able from these stones to raise up children to Abraham. Even now the ax is lying at the root of the trees; every tree therefore that does not bear good fruit is cut down and thrown into the fire.

"I baptize you with water for repentance, but one who is more powerful than I is coming after me; I am not worthy to carry his sandals. He will baptize you with the Holy Spirit and fire. His

winnowing fork is in his hand, and he will clear his threshing floor and will gather his wheat into the granary; but the chaff he will burn with unquenchable fire."

Texts: Isaiah 11:1-10

Psalm 72:1-7, 18-19

Matthew 3:1-12

When the slaves sang "Steal Away," they had in mind getting to Jesus, to the warm, embracing love of his care and value. But, like all oppressed peoples, the slaves knew that religious talk is always inescapably public, political talk. "Stealing Away" was never just a pious hope for communion, but it was also a resolve to escape the harsh exploitation of slavery, an intention to get to a new region where there was another governance of justice, dignity, and freedom. They imagined this other region, under this other governance, to be a version of the kingdom of God. The journey to "Jesus," that is, to the land of freedom and well-being, was indeed hazardous, but they were prepared to sing it and to travel it. Along the way there were many ominous checkpoints before crossing the Ohio River, which symbolized the border into the land of hoped-for freedom.

There was another crossing like that, still memorable to you unless you are very young. It was the most famous crossing between East Berlin and West Berlin, the alleged entry into the freedom and well-being of "the West." It was "Checkpoint Charlie," operated on the Eastern side by rude, ominous border guards, sniffing dogs, and mirrors under cars. You never knew whether you would be permitted to leave—or even to enter, for that matter.

So here we are gearing up for Christmas, imagining that we will "Steal Away to Jesus," the sweet-smelling baby, and away from all

This sermon was preached at Emory University, Atlanta. The texts are from the lectionary for the Second Sunday in Advent.

that is hazardous to our health. We too are on the underground railroad, yearning for a new regime under a better governance, hoping passionately, even romantically, almost forgetting that we have ominous checkpoints on the way, when the stomach tightens and the dogs sniff, and you hold your breath, waiting for the seemingly capricious verdict about entry. It is not "Checkpoint Charlie," for this is not Berlin. And it is not the Ohio River, for this is not slavery and the imagined North. It is rather "Checkpoint John," the Baptizer. The primal truth of Advent is that you cannot get to Jesus except by way of John. You cannot get to the sweet-smelling Jesus of Christmas without checkpoint John, which is as spooky and intimidating as Checkpoint Charlie, or the last gasp of threat before the Ohio River. This text is about the conversation at Checkpoint John. As is characteristic at such checkpoints, John does all the talking. We never get to speak, even to make a self-defense. We only listen to his speech. We are not accustomed to being addressed in this harsh way. So consider John and the border patrol at the edge of the yearned-for kingdom of Jesus:

1. *Concerning John*: "[He] wore clothing of camel's hair with a leather belt around his waist, and his food was locust and wild honey" (Matt. 3:4). John is not user-friendly, not easy and accommodating, not much into church growth. He is dressed in counter-culture clothes, lives close to the street, eats by foraging. His demeanor is not unlike those border patrol people at Checkpoint Charlie—rude, deliberately intimidating, mostly silent and glaring. You put your passport into a slot and it disappears while he checks it. You are totally in his hands and at his mercy. You do not know if your passport will ever again appear.

John's message matches his appearance and his demeanor. He is a baptizer, inviting his listeners to renounce the old government they are leaving, collusion with Rome or tenure or whatever. He says, "You brood of vipers, sneaky, cunning, low-life, poisonous." And we think, "Oh, he has found us out!" This entry point of baptism requires a deep either-or, no compromise, no halfway, no vague boundary. It is either lost or found, dead or alive, free or slave, obedient or accommodating. Which will it be?

2. *Concerning John*: We imagine he wants to know our credentials and our justification for entry. We begin to tell him of our daddy and our daddy's daddy, the one who fought the war, and served the flag, and paid his taxes on time. Our vivid genealogy of credentials and loyalty and privilege goes back forty-two generations, clear to father Abraham.

We say innocently, "you remember my father Abraham—

- the father who was so generous that he gave the good land to his nephew Lot, even though none of it was really his in the first place
- the father who believed the promises of God against all the data . . . until the next chapter when he seized a slave woman in order to acquire an heir
- the father who interceded for Sodom, but to no visible effect
- the father who, in a way we now think barbarous, risked his only beloved son in radical obedience."

Oh, there is much more about him. Yes, that father, we are his children. (We do not even think to mention mother Sarah, so fixed are we on the patrimony of male genes.) The first guy in our family, the best guy, genuinely entitled to entry, even to the forty-second generation, accustomed to privileged access.

This Checkpoint John takes all our credentials and birth certificates and vitae and publication records and all the rest . . . and tears them up! Not interested. At Advent, to the new regime of governance, old inherited virtues and privileges and accomplishments do not count. It dawns on us slowly that admission is neither easy nor automatic. This savage response by the border patrol leads to a hard thought: What then, if not our inherited privilege or our usual priority for access? Christmas being such a wonderful middle-class cultural virtue. What then?

3. *Consider John*: He says, "What then?"

In v. 8 John issues a stern imperative:

Bear fruit worthy of repentance.

Act as though you have changed. Get on with the task. Be productive of the sorts of behavior that belong to your new loyalty. The New Testament is rich in its inventories of the required fruits:

- Love, joy, peace, patience, kindness, generosity, faithfulness, gentleness, self- control (Gal. 5:22)
- Good, right, and true (Eph. 5:9)
- The fruit of righteousness (Phil. 1:11)
- The peaceful fruit of righteousness (Heb. 12:11)
- Fruit of righteousness is sown in peace for those who make peace (James 3:17- 18)

and in our Old Testament readings, the fruit named by Isaiah is to

- judge the poor with righteousness
- decide with equity for the meek of the earth so that
- they will not hurt or destroy on all my holy mountain.

In the royal Psalm 72, we find such fruit:

> may the king defend the cause of the poor of the people,
>   give deliverance to the needy,
>   and crush the oppressor.

This is not a list of stoic virtues nor a catalog of good deeds. This is rather the evidence and consequence of a reoriented life, a life now made so trusting, that the neighbor is no longer a threat or a competitor but a partner in the building of a new community. Act differently, says Checkpoint John, if you want in here, if you want to "Steal Away to Jesus."

That's v. 8. But in v. 10, just two quick verses later, the imperative command of John has turned into a terrible threat:

> Even now the ax is lying at the root of the trees; every tree therefore that does not bear good fruit is cut down and thrown into the fire.

Now it may be that John does not think in a disciplined, linear fashion. It may be that we should take this utterance only as a rhetorical eruption, without much precision. Nonetheless, as it stands, the move to that terrible threat in the speech of John suggests that John's listeners must have produced the fruit of the new governance even before they get to the checkpoint. They are to do the new fruit well before they are evaluated for entry. Act the new way even under pressure in the old regime. The old regime is marked by oppression, exploitation, and greed. Even in that context, be at work for the new devotion to sweet Jesus, even before you have entered his realm, and before you live under the protection of his flag. Otherwise, warns Checkpoint John, you are not only excluded, but cut down and thrown into the fire, to mix the metaphors.

So we live these Advent weeks up to and at the checkpoint. We eagerly look to sweet Jesus and his gift of well-being. But we have work to do that is different from romancing Christmas. Everybody knows this is an odd season and even an odd Christmas. We have been mightily sobered about the world. Our privileged access in the world is now deeply in jeopardy. We no longer trust the economy. The index of homelessness rises close to our houses, and hate grows commensurate to our fear and to our sense of vulnerability.

It is now clear to very many that the old patterns of greed have failed, and cannot produce the humanness for which we yearn. We walk cautiously up to the checkpoint, not knowing what it will require. But we also go there eagerly, hoping for another flag, a changed loyalty, a different governance, wanting to get our lives in order and our common life ordered for well-being. Like those old slaves, we yearn to steal away for something better and more hospitable.

The departure into that freedom, however, is as costly for us as it was for the first departure of our people with Moses:

- away from the flesh-pots to vulnerability
- away from regular food supplies to miracles
- away from advantage to neighbor justice
- away from rage to respect for neighbor
- away from self-hatred to self-respect

- away from the "works of flesh" to the "works of the spirit," from strife, jealousy, anger, greed and all the rest, eligible for entry past the rigors of John.

We are poised, like God's people are always poised, to move ahead or to turn back to business as usual. This checkpoint haunts us, because it reminds us that we could indeed be different and the world could be different. It does not have to stay this wretched way, but the transformation requires leaving and stealing away to the new.

The Gospel story always begins with John quoting Isaiah 40:3:

> Prepare the way of the Lord,
> make straight his paths.

The image presented in the poem is of exiles joyously en route home. You know what? We have never been home yet, to full justice, to full peace, full righteousness, full neighbor-love, full self-love, full trust and obedience. Never there even now. Advent is pondering what it would be like to end our common exile and come home.

19

On the Wrong Side of the Ditch . . . For a Long Time

Luke 16:19-31

"There was a rich man who was dressed in purple and fine linen and who feasted sumptuously every day. And at his gate lay a poor man named Lazarus, covered with sores, who longed to satisfy his hunger with what fell from the rich man's table; even the dogs would come and lick his sores. The poor man died and was carried away by the angels to be with Abraham. The rich man also died and was buried. In Hades, where he was being tormented, he looked up and saw Abraham far away with Lazarus by his side. He called out, 'Father Abraham, have mercy on me, and send Lazarus to dip the tip of his finger in water and cool my tongue; for I am in agony in these flames.' But Abraham said, 'Child, remember that during your lifetime you received your good things, and Lazarus in like manner evil things; but now he is comforted here, and you are in agony. Besides all this, between you and us a great chasm has been fixed, so that those who might want to pass from here to you cannot do so, and no one can cross from there to us.' He said, 'Then, father, I beg you to send him to my father's house—for I have five brothers—that he may warn them, so that they will not also come into this place of torment.' Abraham replied, 'They have Moses and the prophets; they should listen to them.' He said, 'No, father Abraham; but if someone goes to them from the dead, they will repent.' He said to him, 'If they do not listen to Moses and the prophets, neither will they be convinced even if someone rises from the dead.'"

Texts: Psalm 107:1, 33-43
1 Timothy 6:6-19
Luke 16:19-31

Jesus was massively alert to and concerned for the terrible, cynical inequities that beset the human community. He told a story about those inequities to help his hearers think again, even after we are weary of thinking on the subject. It is the story appointed for this Sunday in our lectionary.

There was a rich man. There always is. He is the first mentioned in the story. He is the one who is worth noticing, the one who will claim our major attention. He is, as he is expected to be, the main character. But always in the shadow of the rich man there is this other one, his counterpart, the poor man. They belong together, having something like an interdependent relationship. It is astonishing that whenever we find great wealth it will be shadowed by great poverty.

The first scene is about their life together on earth. It is a short scene, because the action is predictable and not very interesting. Indeed, there is more description here than action. The rich man is dressed in fine linen and eats something like a banquet at every meal. There is nothing for him of "Do not be anxious what you shall eat or what you shall drink." He has none of those worries. He has no anxiety, because his life is good, crowned with mercy and lovingkindness.

There is nothing surprising about the poor man either. He is covered with sores; probably he has no health insurance. He eats the droppings from the table, so weak and defenseless and available that the dogs lick his sores. Even the dogs have no great respect for

This sermon was preached at Trinity Presbyterian Church, University City, Missouri. The texts are from the lectionary for a Sunday late in the Pentecost season.

him. As he always does, Jesus the storyteller draws the contrast sharply, no middle ground, no spillover from one to the other. It is as though a great chasm stands between the rich man and the poor man, and neither is able to reach across it to make contact. The two in fact have nothing in common and no contact.

Well, at least for a while there is nothing in common between them. In an instant, however, they have everything in common. What they have in common overcomes all that was different between them. At the top of v. 7, the poor man dies. You knew he would, quickly and unnoticed, perhaps of infection, or perhaps because of malnutrition, or perhaps simply of neglect. I imagine he was ungrieved and not remembered. By the end of the same v. 7, one phrase later, the rich man dies. It is a moment of dreadful equity, alike for an instant. The first part of the story, the account of their life on earth together, is not very revealing. We all know this much about rich and poor, even without this story. We know that the rich and poor are very different in life, very alike in death.

Only now does the story become interesting, because now the story takes us into the part of their life that we have not yet seen or experienced. The storyteller takes us on ahead of our own lived experience. The most important part of the story begins only now. The crucial element in their life, so Jesus suggests, is the part that remains unseen, and here we are permitted to see what we have not seen. The story is such an odd proposal, odd especially to sophisticated people like us, to suggest that the real stuff of our lives happens after death, beyond our lavish eating and our crumby starving.

Something very strange happens. Appearances no longer count; old advantages are suddenly dysfunctional and irrelevant. On the one hand, the story resists our cool cynicism that "when you're dead you're dead." No trajectory of one's life continues. On the other hand, the story also resists any scare that you will have to pay for petty, little affronts about sex and all of those "values" we hear about so much.

Jesus is a storyteller of considerable range and imagination. He has read the Old Testament, and he knows the theological options that are available for a storyteller. He knows about father Abraham, because he has read the book of Genesis. He knows about singing, "Rock-a My Soul in the Bosom of Abraham." He imagines this embracing, gentle old father who waits at death to embrace well-beloved children, no questions asked, no conditions, no qualifications to meet—just come on home to comfort and warmth and caring. But Jesus had kept reading the old scroll even after Genesis, right into Exodus. He read right on into the terror of Moses at Mt. Sinai with all his harsh, revolutionary requirements. He could still feel the tremble of Moses' demanding "if." *If* you obey, you may come on in to the covenant. *If* you don't obey, duck, because you are in some big trouble. The people who put these ancient texts together noticed that Moses did indeed trust in the promises God had made to Abraham, but there was nothing in Moses of the warm embrace of father Abraham, because the mountain was too severe, and the revolution was so urgent, so nobody ever sang about "Rock-a My Soul in the Bosom of Moses." Moses is too harsh and cold and demanding.

So Jesus brings these old, tense memories into our story of the two dead men. Each dead man receives one dimension of the old faith. The poor man died first. It was the only time in his life he had been first. He is assigned first, to a part of the faith of the Old Testament. Would you believe he is assigned to the bosom of father Abraham, even though I would have thought that that place was reserved for the rich man? He is gathered to that caring bosom as his abiding place in the age to come. He is there, dirty, with open sores, but deeply loved in the welcoming embrace of father Abraham.

The rich man, as you know, died too. He had assumed, and I had assumed, that he was the one headed for the bosom of Abraham. Instead, however, we find him quickly, without pause or comment, in the torment of Hades, not the warmth of embrace but the heat of wretchedness. So they are both situated, but neither got what I thought was coming to him.

The poor man never speaks. He is used to not speaking, because the poor learn to keep their mouths shut. And besides, what does he need to say? He got the best part of the old theology. He got the receptivity of Genesis, and he is fully at home. The rich man is stunned, and thinks there must be a mistake. He is accustomed to better reservations, and now has been wrongly assigned to the annex. His request of father Abraham is modest. He asks for mercy. Remember that back before he died, the rich man had not asked for mercy (or anything else), because he did not need it—nor did he grant any. Now the rich man asks a small thing. He asks for Lazarus the poor man to be his water boy, "Come bring some cool water for my burning lips." He asks for it "in the agony of the flames." He is accustomed to summoning the poor man who is always ready to serve, being a member of the pitiful "labor pool." The rich man assumed that the old roles and old patterns of power and domination would continue to operate even here.

Father Abraham, however, knows better. Abraham is firm with the rich man, but he is not unkind. He calls to the rich man, "child." He does not reject him and admits that they are related to each other, albeit remotely. But father Abraham tells him the truth about his situation, the new truth of his life in his changed circumstance. The truth is, you used up your quotas of good stuff, and you get no more. You used your advantage carelessly and insensitively. Lazarus, by contrast, never received much of the good stuff to which he is entitled, has always been entitled, so he has begun on it now, belatedly. This is an astonishing reversal, you in agony, he comforted, so unlike the way it was arranged when the rich man had his way. But death is an extremity, a limit. And there God moves in on things, takes them out of our control, and rearranges life in drastic ways. So the two are positioned, one close to the father of all mercies, and the other one cut off, for the first time in his life, cut off.

No, says father Abraham to the rich man. It is all settled and cannot be renegotiated. There is a deep ditch between his comfort and your agony, the same kind of abyss that used to exist between your wealth and his need. I cannot reach across to you nor bring water for your parched lips. You cannot come over here, no bosom for your discomfort. There the ditch is. It's settled now. In fact, it was settled since you were rich and indifferent, and he was poor and neglected. You of course did not know it, but even then you were settling your long-term choice of the several theological alternatives that are given in the old scrolls, settled between the gentleness of Genesis and the exacerbation of Exodus.

The rich man is in character; he does not bargain nor beg. He is used to facing reality, so he lets it be. He knows he is destined to be on the wrong side of the ditch, far away from water, comfort, or relief. But he is also a family man, with family values. He no longer thinks of himself, but only of his brothers, five of them. It's too late for me, but it's not too late for them. If only they can find out that the hidden stuff after death is the more crucial and risky matter.

In our hearing of the story, we are closest to the role of the brothers. For us, like the brothers, it is not too late, if only we can be adequately warned. So the rich man proposes to father Abraham, "Send them Lazarus." It did not work to have Lazarus bring water, but this is a more noble task. If only the brothers can get a wake-up call before it is too late, so that they can look again at this rich-poor business. "I only acted as I did because I did not know any better. Unwarned, I did what everyone else was doing."

But father Abraham is so unaccommodating. "No, Lazarus will not go on your errand. No. Lazarus is comfortable here, and I am not going to disturb his well-earned rest. No more messengers. The messenger has already been sent, a long time ago."

"What is that? Oh, you mean Moses, hard, tough, unaccommodating Moses."

"The message was:

> Thou shalt not worship other gods.
> Thou shalt not make images out of your stuff.
> Thou shalt not steal.
> Thou shalt not covet.
> Love your neighbor."

"I never understood that was a message, and I certainly never took it as a warning. I thought it was just a bunch of rules for concrete operational people who were not too far along on the faith journey toward self-actualization. Send somebody else."

"No, nobody else will be sent."

So the last scene we have in this little story is of Lazarus held close, basking in the wondrous tradition of Abraham: the rich man, set in the context of harsh Moses, wiping his feverish brow, endlessly, trapped on the wrong side of the ditch, cut off from all forms of life and hope.

This is a hard, demanding story. I would not dare tell it to you, mostly strangers to me, except it is the text picked for us long ago in the church. But then, it's only a story, not more, not a blueprint, not advice, not a scare, not an urging or a scolding. And besides,

There is nothing here about what one must do,

- nothing here about being liberal or conservative
- nothing here about "welfare" or "the private sector"
- nothing here about how to vote or spend or share or save.

The story does not ask anyone to do anything. For who among us could entertain the notion that the important stuff in our life begins only afterward? Who would imagine that there is a ditch cast across our life, holding the potential for cutting us off from all that we treasure? Who would think that the truth of Moses is enough, when there is the better, wondrous truth of Abraham?

It is enough to see that the Bible lives in a terrible tension between tender father Abraham and tough Moses who gives only apodictic clues without explanation. The word is that we have already been warned. What the story does is to reframe our economic life, in a world of haves and have-nots, into a context of long-term division, as though decisions about our wealth and poverty were of eternal significance. Almost all of us, I imagine, are on the surplus side. Here life is reframed to assert that our indifference to neighbor matters to eternity, matters in the ultimate calculus and shape of our life. Our common talk of religion and politics and economics is mostly about safe things, but here it comes down to food and hunger, to linen clothing and licked sores.

Jesus, this terrible storyteller, gives us a zinger. There is nothing to do with a story but to be haunted by it, haunted in this age and in the age to come, haunted at feast and in poverty, haunted through hope and midst warning. We baptized have agreed to host the haunting and to be crowded by it.

While you are haunted, consider this very odd fact. The poor man is remembered. We know his name, Lazarus, as does even father Abraham. The rich man never had a name or an identity. He had only a social role that was temporary and did not last. He is forgotten, unnamed, and abandoned. No name, and no comfort, no future, no water. His future haunts our present.

20
The Threat of Life: Permitting Its Intrusion

Luke 20:27-38

Some Sadducees, those who say there is no resurrection, came to him and asked him a question, "Teacher, Moses wrote for us that if a man's brother dies, leaving a wife but no children, the man shall marry the widow and raise up children for his brother. Now there were seven brothers; the first married, and died childless; then the second and the third married her, and so in the same way all seven died childless. Finally the woman also died. In the resurrection, therefore, whose wife will the woman be? For the seven had married her."

Jesus said to them, "Those who belong to this age marry and are given in marriage; but those who are considered worthy of a place in that age and in the resurrection from the dead neither marry nor are given in marriage. Indeed they cannot die anymore, because they are like angels and are children of God, being children of the resurrection. And the fact that the dead are raised Moses himself showed, in the story about the bush, where he speaks of the Lord as the God of Abraham, the God of Isaac, and the God of Jacob. Now he is God not of the dead, but of the living; for to him all of them are alive."

Texts: 1 Chronicles 29:10-13
Psalm 148
2 Thessalonians 2:13-3:5
Luke 20:27-38

The people in the Gospel narrative could smell the danger in Jesus. They needed only sniff the air around him or notice the people who traveled with him to sense the threat. They had life arranged about the best way it could be. Jesus came into their midst as a threat of newness and deep change and massive transformation. Everywhere Jesus went, by his words and by his acts he caused newness to emerge. He caused old things to drop off and die. He even dismissed some of what people most treasured.

In Luke 20, those most threatened by Jesus, those with the most to lose, the scribes, priests, elders, and Pharisees, quiz him and try to trick him by a series of questions to show either that he is crazy and irrelevant or to establish that he is dangerous as an enemy of the system. First they ask him about his authority (v. 2), and then they ask him if it is proper to obey Roman law (v. 22). These are dangerous questions. He answers enigmatically.

Then, in our lesson for the day, come the most threatened and the most frightened, the Sadducees. They are the big downtown priests who are cozy with the governors and emperors and bankers. They traffic in power. They are the pushers and movers who have learned to compromise, and they know how to get things done. They realistically live in this world, as this is the only world there is or will be. It is as good as it can ever be, and we must keep it and maintain it. They do not want change, certainly not the kind that Jesus offers, because they notice that "the people," the ones they try to keep in their place, are getting uppity around Jesus.

But you can't ask about that directly, for that would show your own fear and your own vested interest. So they must take high ground as the defenders of the Torah. They do not want to show that Jesus is their enemy. What they want to show is that Jesus is an enemy

This sermon was preached to a coalition of Lutheran parishes in Eugene, Oregon.

of the Torah, of the tradition, of the sacred trust of Moses, whereas they are the true conservatives who conserve the old conviction.

So they ask Jesus a question about the Torah. Perhaps it is a cynical question; maybe it is partly serious. Likely they want some assurance from him. They know the kinds of dangerous sounds he is making about transformation and they come to ask, You are not going to change everything, are you? So they quote Deuteronomy 25 to him. How odd that with all the questions about life and faith and power swirling around them they find in the text a rather marginal issue for oppressed Jews in the first century. The law from Moses had said that if a man dies without a son his brother must marry his widow and bear a son so that the name of the dead brother should survive to the next generation. They pushed this instruction to its exaggerated extreme. This must be done up to the seventh brother if need be, for it is important to keep the family name and identity. The law intends to guard continuity in families and tribes. The law is for the strengthening of the family. It may seem to us an odd practice, but it makes sense in a certain social setting.

But these religionists push the law beyond its plain meaning and real intent. They are the main voice in Judea that does not believe in the resurrection. They do not believe that God can do a new thing. They think their old rules will cover all eventualities and if the new eventuality violates the law, it cannot be. The old law is more precious than any new emergent in life. How frightened can they be? So they ask, if these seven brothers all have had this same wife, and they are all raised from the dead (which we do not believe, but you do), which one in the day of resurrection will have the woman for a wife? This resurrection business makes the law unworkable. Jesus is trapped. He does not want to violate the Torah, but he is committed to this notion that God will do a new thing. It is the perfect trap of religious tradition in conflict with powerful, evangelical hope. Surely God will do nothing that runs beyond our tight religious control.

They sense, as Jesus surely knew, that resurrection is dangerous business. It is not just about the dead person being resuscitated. It is about God's power for life that moves into all our arrangements, shatters all our categories by which we manage, control, and administer. It speaks about God's will for new life working where we thought our tired deathliness would prevail. And the Sadducees plead: Please tell us that such dangerous life will not come among us.

Jesus' answer is more massive, more radical, more dangerous than they had imagined. Of all things, he refers to the burning bush of Exodus 3 to say, You can see already there that Moses believes in the resurrection because God there refers back to Abraham, Isaac, and Jacob. Jesus is saying, I can play your silly Bible games and I can out-Bible you, and I am on the side of Moses. Now that is a doubtful argument, but it is adequate to get the conversation started. But then Jesus moves on past such empty Bible quoting (because all of us can quote the Bible any way we want). Jesus refuses to engage in their tricky reasoning and will not participate in a numbers game about one wife and seven husbands. What he tells them is that the power of the resurrection is so massive, so overwhelming, so utterly new, so beyond our categories, that we are not going to discuss this numbers game; it is all irrelevant. In the new age, when the rule of God breaks through, all the categories through which we try to explain and control life and keep it in tow for our purposes are simply pushed aside. Because all our posturing to keep it under control breathes the air of death and finally kills and cheapens and mocks the power of life.

Then he shifts the subject. If you want to talk about Moses and Torah and marriages and one and seven and husbands, and all of that, you can, but I will not linger there. He quickly dismisses all this and he speaks about God whom he knows so well and whom we confess he embodies. Of course there is a resurrection. Of course there is a coming new age. Of course the power for life will prevail. Of course the world will not fit into our little categories. And this is true, not because of magic or tradition or Torah. It is true because of the character and purpose and faithfulness of God who will make all things new. He then delivers the central message:

Now he is not God of the dead, but of the living;
for all live to him.

He is the power of life in the midst of a world bent on death.

In that moment all the cunning questions of the Sadducees are nullified. And the story ends with the scribes saying, "Teacher, you have spoken well. For they no longer dared to ask him a question." We are there at the center of things and the Sadducees could sense it. We are at the main truth of God. God wills life. God has power for life. God will work life among us. All our political, moral, theological tinkering around the edges does not touch the main truth of God that God gives new life which shatters all our ways of control. We are here at the main truth of our own life. The God of life wills life for us. You see, Jesus refuses to let the resurrection be carried off into future speculation. It concerns us here and now. It concerns our readiness to receive new life. We become aware, as did the contemporaries of Jesus, that with Jesus we are placed in crisis with all the old patterns of death we so much cherish but which day by day are killing us.

Now this is a hard word to us, insofar as we are children of the Sadducees. For those of us who traffic in the church with our little truths, for those of us who live in the scientific community and imagine we will be saved by our knowing, for those who live in the university and have such great confidence in our reason, this is a hard word, because it announces that the management of our life is beyond us and we can feel undone.

But the hard word is a good word. Take another sniff of Jesus. What smelled like threat, if we pay attention, smells like new possibility. What we sense to be a deep shattering can also be a beginning again. The power of God for life, the power of the resurrection is the breaking of the vicious cycles of death. It is so in our world, where we live under the threat of nuclear death; the power of the resurrection among us is at work against that insanity. All around us the power of the resurrection is breaking out against oppression, and the old weary categories of bondage, intolerance, and brutality are now called into serious question. The news is that God's power for life will not be overridden or resisted or defeated. Close to home, the cold despair of our deathliness will be overcome. God will have God's say.

We can respond in threat. But we can also respond in thanksgiving and delight. The Sadducees no doubt went home mumbling and waiting for another day in which to trap Jesus. But our text from 1 Chronicles gives us another model for how to regard this God of the living. David is an amazing model of faith for us, for David did not grovel in the loss of his controlling categories. He is portrayed regularly as one who could trust, who could repent, who could risk, who could change. In this text, at the culmination of his life, he is a creature of unfettered praise, and he invites the whole community of faith to praise with him. His words portray the handing of life willingly over to God. One notices the preponderance of words that point toward God:

> Thine O Lord, is the greatness, the power, the glory, the victory, the
> majesty; for all that is in the heavens and in the earth is thine;
> thine is the kingdom. Thou art exalted as head above all.
> In thy hand are power and might; in thy hand it is to make
> great and to give strength. We thank thee. We praise your name.
> (1 Chron. 29:11-13)

You, you, your, your, thy, thine. David has his life reordered so that the initiative for life has been ceded over, and he gladly relinquishes the control that the Sadducees so grudgingly try to hold on to.

In Psalm 148 (which has traditional linkages to David), his glad praise of new life is pushed in a cosmic direction. Now the power for life concerns not just us in our private despair or us in our community fear, but the whole world is now claimed for doxology. The whole world is engaged in celebrative acknowledgment that God gives life. The song of life to the God of the living goes like this:

> Praise the Lord!
> Praise the Lord from the heavens;
>   praise him in the heights!
> Praise him, all his angels,
>   praise him, all his host!

The Threat of Life: Permitting Its Intrusion 149

Praise him, sun and moon;
　　praise him, all you shining stars.
Praise him you highest heavens,
　　you waters above the heavens praise him. . . .
Praise the lord from the earth
　　you sea monsters and all deeps,
fire and hail, snow and frost,
　　stormy wind fulfilling his command.
Praise him, praise him, praise him.

The grudging of fearful religionists is broken open in glad acknowledgment. At last the world is seen clearly. The governance of God is not threat but invitation, not danger but possibility.

Of course David and all of Israel know that praise does not remove the problems, does not end obligation, does not terminate the requirement of taking care of widows in the family. But the context is changed, and changed context reframes our way to be present and responsible.

All these texts bear witness to the power of God for new life. That is why we are here. God is at work giving new life. The question is how to receive it. We can receive it fearfully like the Sadducees and hold on to the old rules that give us petty assurance. Or we can turn loose in praise and thanksgiving and doxology, knowing that the power for life and the gift of life overwhelms our fear and our despair.

God's power for life rightly leaves us speechless. We can be speechless, like the Sadducees, and go back to plot how to stay in control one more day. Or we can be speechless in amazement, like David, able only to say "thou, thou, thine," because we find no words for the new reality.

The power of life is not a religious fantasy. It is a fresh lease on keeping our baptism in the face of injustice and poverty and alienation. It affirms to us that God has not yet quit and God will have God's way. We are on our way with God, rejoicing, praising, surrendering, and obeying. We will then address this age with care and compassion, knowing that the age to come is quite safe in God's mercy.

21

The Surge of Dangerous, Restless Power

Acts 4:5-12

The next day their rulers, elders, and scribes assembled in Jerusalem, with Annas the high priest, Caiaphas, John, and Alexander, and all who were of the high-priestly family. When they had made the prisoners stand in their midst, they inquired, "By what power or by what name did you do this?" Then Peter, filled with the Holy Spirit, said to them, "Rulers of the people and elders, if we are questioned today because of a good deed done to someone who was sick and are asked how this man has been healed, let it be known to all of you, and to all the people of Israel, that this man is standing before you in good health by the name of Jesus Christ of Nazareth, whom you crucified, whom God raised from the dead. This Jesus is

> *'the stone that was rejected by you, the builders;*
> *it has become the cornerstone.'*

There is salvation in no one else, for there is no other name under heaven given among mortals by which we must be saved."

Mostly the world believes all the assets are frozen, and things will stay the way they are. You know: If you're dead, you're dead, and will stay so. And if you are alive, you had better scramble and get it all, because that's all there is and all there is going to be. If you are homeless, you will be that way forever. If you are number one, you had better have lots and lots of power, because that's the way to keep it the way it is. Everything is arranged and settled and fixed and closed; you cannot cross any of these lines, and we work hard to keep the boundaries secure. With this way of reality, some of us end in complacency, because it works to our advantage; some of us end in despair because we had hoped for better, but power operates largely to close things down and keep all the assets frozen.

Against that view, which is dominant among us, Jews and Christians have long sung otherwise. Israel has this very old song, Psalm 98, that asserts that Yahweh is a God of odd, dangerous, surging power in the earth which unsettles and revamps and opens and jeopardizes and heals. The God of the Bible is an inscrutable power for life released in the world. That power breaks down our settlements of rich and poor, of dead and alive, of insiders and outsiders, breaks down our categories of security and explanation, and there are endless, unexpected violations of the categories of the full and the hungry. There is a kind of dangerous restlessness that lets nothing stay fixed and frozen, because God is on the move in more ways than we can understand.

This sermon was preached at the Cathedral of St. Philip, Atlanta.

In the Easter season the church reflects on this riddle of power. While the world basically uses power to shut things down, to silence new possibility, to intimidate newness that threatens, Christians are called to notice the dangerous restlessness of God's power that shatters our complacency and overrides our despair. That restlessness from God makes life possible in our deadness and makes hope possible in our despair, makes healing possible, even in the midst of our hurt and our hate and our fear. People like us are placed in crisis by Easter, because we also prefer to freeze our assets, but the power surges and we notice. No wonder that, in that ancient Psalm about God's odd power, the trees and fields and sea sing for joy, because new life becomes possible wherever the power of this God is at work. This power is unloosed in the world. We are left dazzled, because we did not think it would happen. We are threatened, because we do not want our tea party upset. We are invited, and in any case, we cannot ignore the new power.

The reading for today from the book of Acts is about this dangerous, restless power. Indeed, the whole story of the book of Acts is about this power from God that the world cannot shut down. The book of Acts, in scene after scene, is a hard meeting between the church and worldly authorities, because worldly authorities are regularly baffled by this new power and resentful of it. In our reading, the sequence of the narrative goes back a chapter in the book of Acts.

1. In chapter 3, Peter and John just came out of church, and they saw a lame man. He was begging. He needed money. These two leaders of the church answer, "We have no silver or gold. What we have, we give. In the name of Jesus, stand up and walk" (3:6). And he did! He was seen walking and leaping and praising God. In its monetary poverty, without resources, the church was a carrier of God's power for new life. The story does not explain how this could happen, indeed, doesn't even indicate curiosity. It is enough to wit-

ness to the newness that has been seen, a newness that lets full humanness come, even into a world filled with disability.

2. Predictably, the crowds come around the oddity, partly in curiosity, partly wanting more help, partly upset and resistant. They are upset because for them everything was known and explained, and this new power shattered all their controlling categories. They were "utterly astonished," for they now had seen something they knew was impossible. They saw a broken person restored to full humanity, when they knew very well that this lame man could not cross the line from disability to wholeness. They knew that, so they asked with some hostility about the new power.

Peter is never at a loss for words of response to the bewildered crowd:

> Why do you wonder at this, or why do you stare at us, as though by our own power or piety we had made him walk? The God of Abraham, the God of Isaac, and the God of Jacob has glorified his servant Jesus . . . whom God raised from the dead. To this we are witnesses. And by faith in his name, his name itself has made this man strong whom you see and know; and the faith that is through Jesus has given him this perfect health in the presence of all of you.
>
> (Acts 3:12-16)

Peter has no doubt that the power unloosed in Jesus has now come to be present in the lame man. As a result, the lame man no longer respects our controlling categories. He crosses the line from lameness to health. The old arrangement is thereby threatened.

3. While all this is going on, the text says an interesting thing. It says that the leadership of the community was "much annoyed," because they were preaching that in Jesus there is the resurrection of the dead (4:2). Interesting phrase: "They were much annoyed," not curious, not baffled, but upset.

The reason they were annoyed is that the news of resurrection is unsettling. It shatters all our categories. It announces that our control of reality is no longer adequate or functional. It asserts that newness is possible which we cannot predict or manage according to our vested interest. It insists that the world will not be ordered according to our preferences or in the service of our advantages. No wonder they were annoyed!

The resurrection is not just about a dead man come back to life. It is about power at work that we cannot control, power to make human life possible in all the failed places. So consider Easter in the failed places you can identify:

- power that says you do not need to grovel in despair at the failed places in your life any more than that pitiful beggar, because energy is given in the world for your newness. You can violate the old loyalties and reject the old identity that keeps you from newness.
- power unleashed that lets families get past old, disabling quarrels, that lets churches get past silly old resistances, so that the parties to the quarrel may all together do a newness not on the terms of any of them.
- power released among the nations that will stop the attraction of fear and hate and greed and war, power to take a new action that will stop the savage, unproductive hostility. So we get this poet that sounds like Easter:

> swords to plowshares
> spears to pruning hooks,
> nation shall not lift up sword against nation,
> and not learn war any more.
>
> (Isa. 2:4)

This Easter release of power is not a private, spiritual deal. It is a public matter of transformation that takes place in the real world of economics and politics. They were annoyed, because they loved the hostilities and the old quarrels and their dreams of domination and control and advantage. Those who refuse the truth of the resurrection

- prefer the old crippling identities
- prefer the old quarrels and the old silly resistances
- prefer the old patterns of war and hate and greed, hoping to benefit thereby.

The Surge of Dangerous, Restless Power   155

In our annoyance, when we love the old deathly ways, we frontally deny Easter and the power of the resurrection. In our complacency, we prefer our control; in our despair, we think nothing else can happen, and we join the dead and freeze the assets. Thus the early church makes its dangerous witness in a world that is cynical and annoyed.

4. After the healing of the lame man (3:6), and after the "utter astonishment" of the crowds (3:11), and after the annoyance of the leadership (4:2), they lock up the Christians. Indeed, the old powers always lock up the dangerous dreamers of new possibility. Easter is enough to get sent to prison. And they conduct a trial of the prisoners.

The church must give an account of its Easter faith. In Acts 4:7 the prosecutor asks: By what power or by what name did you do this? The authorities ever since Pharaoh in the Old Testament and Herod in the New Testament have recognized that a dangerous power is on the loose, which they cannot administer. The answer is given by Peter, filled with the spirit, powered by freedom, saturated with courage, unintimidated. He says:

> If we are questioned today because of a good deed done to someone who was sick and are asked how this man has been healed, let it be known to all of you . . . that this man is standing before you in good health by the name of Jesus Christ of Nazareth, who you crucified, whom God raised from the dead.
>
> (4:9-10)

Peter voices a minority opinion. It is a dangerous opinion in the courts of the status quo. It is a powerful possibility in the world, and the world continues to be astonished and annoyed.

Easter is not just an ancient oddity. Easter is an unsettling way in the world that continues to have socioeconomic, political, and human implications. Easter is not a "spiritual" event, but a surging of power that touches all of life. The Easter question for us is not whether you can get your mind around the resurrection, because you cannot. Rather the question is whether you can permit in your horizon new healing power, new surging possibility, new gestures to the lame, new ways of power in an armed, fearful world, new risk, new life, leaping, dancing, singing, praising the power beyond all our controlled powers.

In our world, the old ways of greed and hate and fear are about to destroy us. We hate our enemy, and we inevitably die a little. We abuse our neighbor, and we end up in a vicious cycle of abuse. We end lonely and weary, but in control. But now comes a powerful, unimaginable alternative!

The book of Acts is written so that assets need not stay frozen. This witness makes a simple affirmation: power for life is unloosed. It is a generous offer of an alternative. It is given to you. It is a dangerous chance. You can be on the side of the newness that God is now working. All our frozenness cannot stop the newness. Think of us; think of you; think of this church—beyond complacency, beyond despair. Our old habits of deathliness now are emptied of authority, because the new is underway. No more frightened hearts, but hearts alive, bodies restored, communities, families, the world —like the lame man, jumping up, leaping, singing, and praising God. It is the same one who used to sit disabled. It could be us!

CHAPTER 22

A Loser's Powerful Footnote

Acts 15:12-22a

The whole assembly kept silence, and listened to Barnabas and Paul as they told of all the signs and wonders that God had done through them among the Gentiles. After they finished speaking, James replied, "My brothers, listen to me. Simeon has related how God first looked favorably on the Gentiles, to take from among them a people for his name. This agrees with the words of the prophets, as it is written,

> *'After this I will return,*
> *and I will rebuild the dwelling of David, which has fallen;*
> > *from its ruins I will rebuild it, and I will set it up,*
> *so that all other peoples may seek the Lord—*
> > *even all the Gentiles over whom my name has been called.*
> *Thus says the Lord, who has been making these things*
> > *known from long ago.'*

Therefore I have reached the decision that we should not trouble those Gentiles who are turning to God, but we should write to them to abstain only from things polluted by idols and from fornication and from whatever has been strangled and from blood. For in every city, for generations past, Moses has had those who proclaim him, for he has been read aloud every sabbath in the synagogues."

Then the apostles and the elders, with the consent of the whole church, decided to choose men from among their members and to send them to Antioch with Paul and Barnabas.

Texts: Psalm 1
Acts 15:12-22a
1 Corinthians 15:1-11
Matthew 13:54-58

It cannot be demonstrated that James, the brother of our Lord, wrote Psalm 1. But give or take a chronological adjustment, it seems likely that James wrote the psalm, or at least someone like James did it. James must have been a tough, passionate, troublesome pillar of the church. We celebrate that whole company of folk who travel with James in all their moral passion, their utter conviction that life is morally coherent. These people keep reminding the church that how we act matters decisively for the future God will give us.

Biblical faith has arisen out of moral passion which we claim to be rooted in God's own heart. The courage of Moses in Egypt voiced God's sense that injustice that violates human possibility in the long run cannot prevail. At Sinai, as Moses went on and on in Leviticus and Deuteronomy, Israel's moral passion grew and expanded, until it occupied all of life, every meal, every sexual act, every bird's nest, every prayer tassel, every homeless slave, every corpse. All belong to God, all are visited by God's holiness, all must be guarded and attended to and honored.

This company of Jesus in which James travels voices a passionate faith that scholars call "Torah piety." That piety proposes that we be occupied day and night, sitting and standing, going out and com-

---

This sermon was preached at the Episcopal Seminary of the Southwest in Austin, Texas, on the Festival of St. James. I had never really thought about St. James, being completely schooled in the triumph of Paul's theology of grace. It was my unreflective impression that James had been completely routed at the "Council of Jerusalem" in Acts 15. This day in the Episcopal calendar of saints invited me to reexamine the witness of the text.

ing in, with enacting life in its awesome holiness. This enactment of holiness in ordinary things touches everything personal and everything public; there are no zones of exemption.

Moreover, those who live this way prosper. In a dry climate, they are said to be like willows near water, with deep roots and staying power, luxuriant growth and productivity. Rooting life in massive obedience keeps one from being blown away by the troubles of the day. Such folk, this tradition claims, have no severe depression at the infidelities of life, no suicides at the collapse of the dollar, because life is shaped in a deeper nourishment, which is reliable.

Of course, this Torah piety, as always happens to moral passion, hardens and becomes shrill and imperialistic. The very life it intended to nourish is diminished by its starchiness. The agenda of moral buoyancy was tempted to become overly scrupulous. And when this faith, in the person of Paul, came to touch the "goy," the outsiders who were not warmed by Torah piety, a showdown was inevitable. The great Jerusalem dispute was an argument about Torah and gospel, about the promise and diminishment of the commandments, about the delicate linkage between indicative and imperative.

It matters enormously that Paul prevailed and set us on the catholic road of Augustine and Luther and Barth and God's unutterable free love. The good news was not to be held down by scruple. Biblical faith refused a sectarian horizon, and turned out to have enormous elasticity.

In that debate, James is clearly the loser. With good grace, he concedes the main point:

> Therefore I have reached the decision that we should not trouble
> these Gentiles who are turning to God.

> (Acts 15:19)

God is larger than Jewish scruple, and James knows it. God is more gracious and more dangerous than the memory of Moses, and

James freely acknowledges this reality about God. We are not children of excessive scruple. We are free in the world, and free for the world, bound only by the call of the one who loves the world with suffering power.

James' speech of concession, however, breathes the Torah piety of Psalm 1. As a result, James cannot let go in his speech of concession without one powerful footnote. He is like the parent of a teenager who inevitably must warn one more time, "Drive carefully. There is deep danger and powerful destructiveness out there, and you had better pay attention." And if the teenager does not heed, the risks are very great. So James adds his footnote of moral passion and Torah piety to the new freedom in the church.

> But we should write them to abstain only from things polluted by idols and from fornication and from whatever has been strangled and from blood. (v. 20)

The footnote of v. 20 takes back a lot of what was given away in the concession of v. 19. What James thinks he is doing is reducing his scruple to the barest, nonnegotiable minimum:

- *Avoid what is polluted by idols.* James knows that a false core loyalty will contaminate and profane every aspect of life. Thus even Gentiles in their deep evangelical freedom must pay attention to their core loyalty, or life in every aspect will be diminished and distorted. The freedom just granted from scruple does not relieve us from deciding about the core loyalty out from which health comes.
- *Abstain from fornication.* The practice of the most intimate and long-term relations must be maintained by fidelity, because distortion and fraud in such relations will foster a deathly sickness everywhere.
- *Avoid what is strangled and from blood.* No doubt this is a reference to Jewish sacrificial practice; behind that precise cultic act

is the notion of faith practiced in violation of life, the notion that somehow violence is legitimate and it will work to protect our life. James knows better.

So James has his fleeting say. The meeting is moved along without any response to the urging of James. Nonetheless, from this speech James looms large over the Gentile church, and he has not been banished from the text by the victory of the other party. Sometimes James and his ilk are an embarrassment to us in their self-conscious morality. Sometimes the church needs to speak of grace utterly free without qualifying footnote.

For all the lyric of grace, however, we learn over and over that James has it right about the irreducible, nonnegotiable realities of his piety. When the drought comes (as it will) and our throats are made too dry for the large lyrics of grace, when wretchedness is in the earth and we cannot muster doxology, the church falls back on the day-to-dayness of core loyalty, key relations that are honest, and sacrifice that shuns violence. In such seasons, we discover that elemental moral practice keeps life whole.

The church has this love affair with Paul and his good news. James, however, is granted a day every now and then. Paul knows about the moral passion of James and his cruciality for the body. When Paul buoyantly lists the witnesses, he writes:

> He appeared to James, then to the apostles. Last of all as to one untimely born, he appeared also to me.
>
> (1 Cor. 15:7-8)

In the list James is prior to Paul. Moral passion precedes free grace; nurture and discipline come before utter freedom. It is not only that the church must be ecumenical enough to entertain both and tolerate this other opinion. We ourselves inevitably keep reenacting the Jerusalem dispute in our common life and in our personal, most intimate growth. It is not only that we know about both, but that in this bread, we hear Torah as good news, in this wine we encounter moral passion in the presence of our gratitude. Eat the bread, drink the wine, take the scroll, and be

> like trees planted by streams of water
> which yield the fruit in its season,
> and their leaves do not wither,
> in all they do, they prosper.
>
> (Ps. 1:3)